Dr en

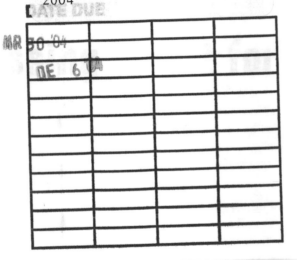

Books by JoAnna Nicholson

Dressing Smart for Men:
101 Mistakes You Can't Afford to Make
& How to Avoid Them

Dressing Smart for Women:
101 Mistakes You Can't Afford to Make
& How to Avoid Them

Secrets Men Have Told Me:
What Turns Men On and What
Turns Them Off

Dressing Smart in the New Millennium:
200 Quick Tips for Great Style

110 Mistakes Working Women Make
& How to Avoid Them:
Dressing Smart in the '90s

How to Be Sexy Without Looking Sleazy

Color Wonderful

Dressing Smart
For Men

101 Mistakes You Can't Afford to Make . . .
and How to Avoid Them

JOANNA NICHOLSON

IMPACT PUBLICATIONS
Manassas, VA

ISBN: 1-57023-199-0

Library of Congress: 2002117047

Publisher: For information on Impact Publications, including current and forthcoming publications, authors, press kits, online bookstore, and sub-mission requirements, visit our website: www.impactpublications.com

Publicity/Rights: For information on publicity, author interviews, and sub-sidiary rights, contact the Media Relations Department: Tel. 703-361-7300, Fax 703-335-9486, or email: info@impactpublications.com.

Sales/Distribution: All bookstore sales are handled through Impact's trade dis-tributor: National Book Network, 15200 NBN Way, Blue Ridge Summit, PA 17214, Tel. 1-800-4626420. All other sales and distribution inquiries should be directed to the publisher: Sales Department, IMPACT PUBLICATIONS, 9104 Manassas Drive, Suite N, Manassas Park, VA 20111-5211, Tel. 703-361-7300, Fax 703-335-9486, or email: info@impactpublications.com.

Layout and Design by Donna B. McGreevy.

Contents

v

Dedication

To all of the stylish men
of my past
present &
future

I am so thankful and honored that my life has been touched by so
many charming,
smart men.

Joseph Caspari, the most stylish and elegant man I know, taught
me that a man is only truly elegant when his behavior toward all
others is always elegant as well.

My awesome, and dashing best friends Aaron, Mehrdad, Len
DePas, and Frank are the most delightful ongoing experiments in
style that a woman could ask for. And whether they are stylish to
the core or wonderful works in progress, Ry, Ricardo, Jean Luc,
Mike, George, Tony, Safa, Ethan, Irwin, William the 1st, William the
3rd, David, Orlando, Bill, Stan, Tom, and Leo are remarkable men
and exceptional friends.

Acknowledgments

When it came to doing the research for this book, my ever stylish and charming friends, Joseph Farnel, founder of J. H. Farnel in Paris, a noted author and award-winning manufacturer of exceptional clothing for men and women that is sold in the finest stores all over the world, and the exceptionally well-dressed William Roberti, the former CEO of Brooks Brothers, and former President and CEO of the Plaid Clothing Group, the second largest tailored clothing manufacturer in the United States whose notable brands include Burberry, had all of the right answers—I will never be able to thank them enough!

A very special thanks to **Macy's**—especially the Tysons Corner, Virginia, store—for allowing me to use their clothing and accessories to help illustrate this book, and to Bruce Nordstrom for graciously agreeing to let me interview many of his top people—especially the very helpful David Shields, manager of men's clothing at Nordstrom in Tysons Corner, Virginia. I am also very thankful to the exceptionally chic Bill Tiefel, the Chairman Emeritus of the Ritz-Carlton hotels; Boudi Hayek at Bernini in the Fashion Center at Pentagon City, Virginia; Pete Kowlessar, the manager of the Men's Wearhouse in Washington, DC; Garrett Drake, the optician at Apex Optical in Washington, DC.; and George Ingram, a personal shopper at Neiman Marcus in Tysons Corner, Virginia, for taking the time out of their busy schedules to give me great answers to my countless questions. I am also grateful to the Industrial Credit Union in Bellingham, Washington, for sharing their dress code with me.

My special thanks and appreciation to **The Photographer's Gallery** in Washington, DC, for the terrific photos that bring the Color 1 concept to life in this book, and I'm eternally grateful to Len De Pas, the unforgettable founder of The Photographer's Gallery, and photographer Paul Zambrana for his exceptional work and comprehension of the "color story" the photos needed to tell. Check out their terrific website at ThePhotographersGallery.net

This book wouldn't exist without my publishers, and my dear friends, Caryl and Ron Krannich—and I am forever appreciative for their belief in me and my life's work. And to Mardie Younglof for her patient and detailed editing.

Dressing Smart for Men

ARE YOU A SMART DRESSER?

Do you look competent or clueless? Great or mediocre? Do you wish you could look like a million bucks without spending a fortune? Do you think anyone is talking behind your back about the way you look? What image do you present when you walk into a room?

If you are like most men, you probably make several dressing mistakes that may visually detract from your competence. Perhaps you have difficulty picking out shirts, ties, suits, and jackets that would make you look fabulous. Or maybe you let someone else (your significant other or salesperson) make those critical decisions for you!

The way you dress sends instant messages about who you are. Right or wrong, you are judged first by the way you look instead of by what you know and who you are. Look great and you'll look like you know most everything. Look like you don't have a clue and you'll look like you don't know anything—even if you have a Ph.D.

One negative impression at the wrong moment can hinder your career. One instant positive image could change your life. A quick look at any man can convey the following:

- Appropriate or inappropriate

- Decision maker or invisible

- Creative or cookie cutter mentality

- Poor, rich, or somewhere in between

- Careful or careless

- Smart, not so smart, or doesn't have a clue

Dressing Smart for Men is your passport to good taste—not for just appropriate looks but for great easy elegant attire regardless of your job, budget, age, or size. It's designed to help you develop an eye for dressing your very best for all occasions. Outlining 101 mistakes you can't afford to make, the following pages offer sage advice on how you can quickly become your own expert so you can dress smart for both work and play. Each mistake is examined and tips provided so you can avoid mistakes in the future.

If you are uncertain what dressing mistakes you make, start by taking the following True/False quiz:

WHAT'S YOUR DRESSING I.Q.?

1. The way you look has nothing to do with helping you get a job or a promotion.   T   F

2. A good person to ask for accurate advice on what goes with what is a salesperson in the men's department.   T   F

3. If you are really good at your job, you won't need to follow a dress code as closely as the next guy.   T   F

4. If your workplace is business casual, it's not important to wear a jacket.   T   F

5. Ties that have muted, quiet, subtle colors look better on men than those that have brighter colors.   T   F

6. Any shade of gray is a good, safe, elegant choice for your suits, jackets, and trousers.   T   F

7. A black suit is a bit formal looking for the office.   T   F

8. A blue shirt will look great with any tie that has blue in it.   T   F

9. All dark-haired men will look better in different colors and color combinations than those that look great on light-haired men.   T   F

10. When it comes to looking professional, a pure white shirt with a dark suit is the best way to go.   T   F

11. To look like you know your "stuff," it's important to keep up with at least some of the latest trends.   T   F

12. To look more intelligent it's important not to wear any of the latest trends.   T   F

13. Never unbutton your jacket during an interview or a very important meeting.   T   F

14. All plain looking leather lace-up shoes are appropriate with all suits.   T   F

15. It's fine to wear a button-down shirt with any suit.   T   F

16. All ties, as long as they are tied in a medium size or smaller knot, can be worn with a button-down shirt.   T   F

17. Men who are fuller-bodied in their midsection should avoid double-breasted jackets.   T   F

18. A white shirt is always appropriate with any suit.   T   F

19. A short-sleeved dress shirt is appropriate with a suit when it is very warm outside.   T   F

20. A shirt with a longer pointed collar is a good choice for a man with a round face who wishes to make his face look less round.   T   F

21. A dressy looking tie can "dress-up" a more casual looking suit.   T   F

22. During an interview the person doing the interviewing will make a judgment about whether you look right for the job in just 15 seconds.   T   F

23. Khakis with a polo shirt is a good choice for a business casual look.   T   F

24. If your co-workers wear jeans and T-shirts to work, it's okay for you to do the same.   T   F

25. It's not a good idea to call attention to yourself because of what you are wearing.   T   F

26. Looking totally coordinated all of the time could hurt your image.   T   F

27. It's old fashioned to think that your shoes need to always match your belt.   T   F

28. It's being overly picky to worry about matching the metals of your belt buckle, blazer buttons, watch, and cuff links.   T   F

29. Your suits, jackets, and trousers should be dry cleaned frequently.   T   F

30. Moths don't/won't eat holes in clothing that has been dry-cleaned just before storing or that is stored with cedar chips, in a cedar closet, or cedar chest.   T   F

31. It's okay to travel in very casual attire (like sweats and athletic shoes) as long as you don't have to go straight into a meeting when you arrive.   T   F

   If you answered "True" to any of the above statements, you should find this book useful. The short response to each statement should be "False." The remainder of this book provides details on each of these mistakes. The quick and easy answers to each of the above statements are as follows:

ANSWERS

1. False—it can be a tie breaker or even an enormous help.

2. False—the vast majority of salespeople are not trained and many will offer an opinion that is often wrong.

3. False—even if you are very, very good at what you do, the way you look can hold you down or help move you up.

4. False if you want to get ahead—the simple act of wearing a jacket when you don't have to can give you an important edge.

5. False for about 50% of you—there is a 50/50 chance that wearing muted, quiet colors can make you look ineffective.

6. False—there are many shades of gray (from blue grays to brownish grays) and only one or two will look great on you—the others could make you look drab.

7. False—if you look great in black you can wear it anywhere.

8. False—to look good, the blues need to be from the same color family.

9. False—the colors and color combinations that will look super on you have to do with your Color Type, and of the 12 different Color Types, dark-haired men can be found in all 12 and light-haired men in 6 of the 12.

10. False for about 50% of you. It's a 50/50 chance that pure white (especially when worn with a dark suit) will look inexpensive on you while a softer white will look great.

11. False—you can dress in totally classic attire and look awesome.

12. False—if you choose carefully, wearing a trend could make you look brilliant (or at least savvy).

13. False—it's fine to unbutton your jacket when seated and button it when you stand up.

14. False—lace-ups that are heavy looking are not appropriate with light/tropical weight suiting fabrics.

15. False—button-down shirts are too casual looking to be worn with dressy suits, especially pinstripes.

16. False—dressy looking ties look out of place on button-down shirts.

17. False—double-breasted styles can look great on anybody—it's all in the way they fit.

18. False—suits and jackets that are muted or blended looking most often need to be worn with a cream, beige, or ecru shirt.

19. False—there is no such thing as a short-sleeved *dress* shirt.

20. False—longer pointed collars are not very flattering to any face shape and instead of making a round face look less round, by contrast, they can make it look more so.

21. False—wearing a silky, dressy looking tie with a casual suit doesn't dress it, or you, *up*—it only makes you look like you don't know what's what.

22. False—it only takes 7 seconds.

23. False unless you want to look like every other man (who has no imagination).

24. False for the same reason as above—at least add a jacket and make sure the T-shirt you are wearing is very nice.

25. False—if you want to move up, it's much better for you in all ways to be memorable than to be invisible.

26. False—having a pulled-together look in your attire indicates to others that you are competent in other aspects of your life as well.

27. False if you want a well-coordinated look and very false if you want a dressy look.

28. False—take the time to match your metals.

29. False—dry cleaning kills your clothes—about three times a season is usually enough.

30. False—dry cleaning or cedar in any amount will not keep moths from eating wool.

31. False—understand really, really well that comfort and sloppy are not synonyms, and that everywhere you go you represent yourself and your company—you never know when your seat mate on an airplane might be the CEO of a company you've always wanted to work for or the woman of your dreams.

101 Mistakes You Can't Afford to Make!

 ## Instant Impression

1 Looking like one of the pack instead of the leader.
2 Believing bad advice.
3 Not looking promotable.
4 Not looking elegant.
5 Looking great one day but not the next.
6 Not knowing how to package yourself.
7 Not caring enough about how you look.
8 Dressing too casually for your place of business.
9 Not looking stylish.
10 Not understanding the look of your industry.
11 Not following, or not understanding, dress codes.

Color Power

12 Not knowing how to use color effectively.
13 Wearing colors that are too bright or too quiet looking on you.
14 Wearing shades of colors that muddy, sallow, or gray your skin causing you to look ineffective or ill.
15 Not knowing how to combine colors in such a way that they flatter you.

 ## Changing the Way the World Looks at You

16 Looking as if you don't have a clue.
17 Not being able to look in the mirror and tell if something isn't working.
18 Not knowing how to work with a tailor.
19 Wearing your jacket sleeves too short or too long.

20 Not owning the perfect suit.

21 Not knowing what to wear to the most important meeting of the year.

22 Wearing suits in stripes that overpower you, causing you to look washed-out, or wearing suits in colors/tweeds or patterns that are weak looking on you, causing you to look drab.

23 Wearing the wrong color shirt and/or tie with your suit, jacket, or blazer.

24 Wearing your jacket too long or too short.

25 Wearing jackets that are too small in the hips so your vents spread.

26 Not knowing which jacket buttons to wear open or closed.

27 Combining patterns in suits and shirts that don't jive.

28 Wearing your trousers below your waist.

29 Wearing your trousers too short.

30 Wearing trousers that don't coordinate with your jacket.

31 Wearing trousers that are too tight, causing the pleats and/or pockets to spread open.

32 Wearing a white shirt with just any suit and tie.

33 Wearing the wrong color shirt for your tie.

34 Showing too much cuff below your jacket sleeve.

35 Wearing short-sleeved shirts as dress shirts.

36 Wearing the wrong color shirt for your coloring.

37 Wearing shirts that have the wrong style/size collar for your neck and face.

38 Wearing a button-down collar with a dressy suit.

39 Wearing ties that don't look good with your shirt and/or suit.

40 Tying your tie too short or too long.

41 Wearing ties that are too bright for you, or ties that look washed-out on you.

42 Wearing pedestrian looking ties.

43 Tying the wrong style or size knot for your shirt collar style.

44 Wearing the wrong width tie for your suit and/or your neck or face.

45 Letting your shirt and/or tie show beneath your vest.

46 Not knowing how to get a great casual elegant look without wearing a tie.

47 Not knowing how to create super looks on a minimal budget.

48 Wearing worn-out, faded-out, or stretched-out polo shirts for business casual attire.

49 Wearing a belt that is casual looking with a dressy suit.

50 Wearing the wrong color belt.

51 Wearing penny loafers with a dressy suit and tie.

52 Wearing the wrong style shoes.

53 Wearing the wrong color shoes.

54 Wearing the wrong color socks.

55 Having part of your bare leg show when you sit down and/or cross your legs.

56 Wearing socks that are too thin looking for your trousers and/or shoes.

57 Dressing too casually for business casual days.

58 Not understanding how to create appropriate and great looking outfits for business casual.

59 Wearing a dressy looking tie with khakis or other casual looking fabrics.

60 Not knowing what to wear for business casual when you don't want to dress-down.

61 Not knowing what to wear to the least important meeting of the year.

62 Not knowing what to wear to a casual get-together at the home of a co-worker.

63 Dressing in your off hours in such a way that it reflects badly on you or your company.

64 Not having the knowledge you need to pull your look together.

65 Dressing too casually or not knowing how to dress for an interview.

66 Not knowing what to wear to your 2nd interview or final interview.

67 Not knowing what to wear on your first day on the job, your first week on the job, or your first day of the 2nd week on the job.

68 Wearing a sporty watch with a dressy suit.

69 Wearing a belt and braces at the same time.

70 Letting too much of your pocket square show.

71 Using a pocket square that is the same exact pattern as your tie.

72 Not matching metals of belt and shoe buckles, blazer buttons, eyeglass frames, and cuff links.

73 Carrying an inexpensive looking pen.

74 Wearing eyeglass frames in unflattering colors.

75 Wearing glasses in unbecoming shapes/styles.

76 Carrying a wallet that makes a non-business statement.

77   Carrying anything that makes a bulge in your pockets.

78   Wearing jewelry inappropriate for your place of business.

79   Carrying a canvas backpack with a suit.

80   Carrying luggage that makes a bad arrival or departure statement.

81   Wearing snow-shoveling gloves or a warm scarf that would look more appropriate at a football game with your business attire.

82   Wearing a casual hat with business attire.

83   Carrying an umbrella that looks as though it barely survived the last storm.

SMALL DETAILS WITH A BIG IMPACT

84   Dressing down at the wrong time.

85   Dressing too casually when you are traveling.

86   Not knowing what to wear when you are traveling and being met/ picked up by someone whose respect you want.

87   Wearing your hair in a style that isn't flattering to you.

88   Wearing clothing that has seen a better day.

89   Not hanging your clothes properly.

90   Over dry-cleaning your clothing.

91   Pressing, instead of steaming, your jackets and pants.

92   Not polishing your shoes.

93   Wearing run-down looking shoes.

94   Not knowing what to wear to a dinner party at your boss's home.

95   Sending the wrong message with your image.

96   Not knowing what to put with what to formulate your own sense of style.

97   Not understanding how to build a good working wardrobe.

98   Not organizing your existing wardrobe.

99   Not knowing when, and when not, to shop with a girl friend, wife, or other friend.

100   Not knowing what to buy first.

101   Not organizing, coordinating, or integrating your new purchases into your wardrobe.

> Look great and you'll look like you know most everything.
> Look like you don't have a clue and you'll look like you don't know
> anything—even if you have a Ph.D. — JoAnna

INSTANT IMPRESSION

One negative impression at the *wrong* moment could hinder your career. One instant positive image could change your life. You never know just when you might run into "fate" in the form of a person who has the power to make your life different. Always be dressed for the part you want to play for the next five years of your life. Use clothing as a tool—think of learning to dress well as a necessary skill that is needed to get the job you want, the future you desire.

The way you dress sends an instant message about who you are—you just want to make sure that you are sending the message you want people to receive. One quick look at any man can convey the following:

- Competent or doesn't have a clue
- *Smart*, not so smart, or dopey
- Creative or cookie cutter mentality
- Caring or not
- Interested or disengaged
- Poor, rich, or somewhere in between
- Decision maker or invisible
- Careful or careless
- Appropriate or inappropriate
- Entry level, worker bee, middle management, or executive

If you tie your tie too short or too long, you could appear dopey and you're definitely not rich, smart, or a decision maker. Perhaps worse, you look like you are a careless person.

Yes, you really "said" all that and all you did was tie your tie! Do you at least still look *appropriate*, because, after all, you **are** wearing the business *uniform* of suit, shirt, and tie? Yes, you look appropriate to play the role of the "goofy" guy in a movie or sitcom.

11

One of the fashion-savvy men I interviewed for this book told me a story about the Emperor Napoleon and a childhood friend of his. They used to "hang out" when they were boys and they stayed friends through the years. When Napoleon became the Emperor he invited his old friend for dinner. His friend, a regular kind of guy with a regular type of job, put on the best clothes that he had. Arriving at Napoleon's house, he presented his invitation at the door but was turned away, being told that he wasn't properly attired to have dinner with the Emperor. He went home, borrowed some "finery" from a neighbor, and returned. This time he was allowed to enter.

Everyone was seated for dinner and the soup was served. Napoleon's old friend started dipping his long lace sleeve into the soup and people were aghast! Everyone took a peek at the Emperor to see what he would do. "Just a minute," he said, "I've known this guy for a very long time and there must be a reason why he is doing this; let's hear what he has to say." His old friend explained that he had come to dinner and been turned away because of what he was wearing and that when he returned wearing a borrowed suit he was admitted. So, since it was the suit that was welcome for dinner, he felt that it was the suit that should have the soup.

> Right or wrong, you are first JUDGED by the way you look instead of by what you know and what kind of person you are. You have to look the part or you may not get to play the role. — JoAnna

In this book you will find that I "talk" to you about looking great—the purpose of this highly detailed text is to serve as a reference guide to show you how. Much more than just a book that advises you to wear a dark suit, white shirt, and conservative tie, or a polo shirt and khakis, you are shown how to put this information into practice to give you an **edge**—higher odds that you will reach your career and personal aspirations.

HAVING AN EDGE N

OVER THE OTHER GUY

JUST THE BASICS

    N   When it comes to color and color combinations, as in most things, you can't believe everything you see, read, or hear.

BEYOND THE BASICS

If what you are wearing is appropriate and it fits well, there is only one reason why you might not look good—the colors you are wearing. Either your colors don't work together, or they are making you appear insignificant, washed-out, or like you aren't feeling very well.

> Ø **Bad *advice is rampant*!** When it comes to color and color combinations, don't believe everything you read or see in books and magazines or hear from sales personnel, your significant other, or your best friend. Significant others and best friends you may understand, but when it comes to "experts," surely I must not know what I'm talking about because why would they showcase something that wasn't correct. Why should you believe what I say? When you have trained your eye to see what works for *you*—or not—you will embrace my advice.

I wish that I could tell you otherwise, but magazine fashion editors, stylists, salespeople, and other "experts" continue to give really bad advice about color, and often about style. Why? For one main reason. Just because a person writes about fashion or sells clothing, doesn't mean that he or she has had any color training or even wardrobe training.

Absorb and practice all of your *dressing smart* tips and train your own eye so that YOU can decide whether to copy a look you see or to follow advice. When you've trained your eye, you can take charge of what you wear *from a color standpoint* and you'll learn to recognize when something looks great on you and, if it doesn't, you will know why. Until you do train your eye, you are **susceptible** to misleading words and pictures.

Here and there in this book you will see the words **"Bad Advice."** The examples are all from books and magazines written to advise men on their wardrobe. My contradiction will follow the bad advice—please don't get them mixed up. The following is the first example:

> Ø **Bad Advice:** Wear a brown, blended looking, houndstooth check suit, a brown and gold tie (sounds okay so far, but wait), with a bright blue and white stripe shirt and a navy and white dot pocket square.

> ① **My Advice:** If you wear this haphazard color combination, you are sending a strong signal that you don't know what you are doing. The shirt and pocket square work together as do the suit and tie—but all together it's an uncoordinated mishmash. To call this attire "creative" is a stretch—it's just a bad color combination.

What man would be foolish enough to wear this bizarre outfit? Hopefully not you, but it was shown as "do" in an expensive wardrobe book for men.

Who am I to give advice on color and color combinations and why take **my** advice instead of "theirs"? I'm one of the founders of the image and color consulting industry, and for 25 years my company, Color 1 Associates,

International Image and Style Consultants, has been training color and wardrobe consultants all over the world. We specialize in helping our clients make a great instant impression—over and over.

It takes only a few seconds to form an opinion about someone. The trouble is, if the opinion, the *impression*, is a bad one, it can take weeks, months, or years to reverse. Our clients can't afford to get it wrong. They include a president, ambassadors, cabinet secretaries, senators, congressmen, Fortune 500 companies, rock stars, Miss Americas, an academy award nominee, and men like you.

When you want to get it right every time, the most important skill you can learn is how to combine the colors of your suits (or jackets and trousers) with your shirts and ties in a way that gives **YOU** a great look. This skill is not just one of learning what works with what, but learning what makes **YOU** appear successful, healthy, and effective. When you master this art, you will have an *edge* over everyone who doesn't know how.

Many men don't care much about clothes and that's fine, but since you are reading this book, I'll assume that you do care about the way you look. If you think that you have the "uniform" down pat and you don't need to learn this additional skill, you may continue through life looking good just from the neck down. And, from the neck up, you may look washed-out, like you don't feel so well, or simply come across as ineffective—not an image that will help you move ahead.

Learning this new skill now will serve you well for the rest of your life. Read about it, understand it, integrate it, enjoy the compliments and the feelings and success that being self-assured will bring. Looking exceptional every day will become second nature to you—you'll get up in the morning, get dressed with ease and elegance, forget about the way you look, and get on with your day, and your life.

There is a very strong color section in this book because *color* is the missing link that makes the difference between your looking bad, okay, or fabulous. Any man can just put on a suit, shirt, and tie and get on with it. You need to train your eye to see what works with what and what looks super on **YOU**.

LOOK PROMOTABLE NOW

JUST THE BASICS

♣   If you don't look the part, you may not get the role.

♣   If you are feeling overwhelmed, confused to the point that you won't absorb the information in this book, or if you don't have the time right this minute to do anything but get to a store and buy a suit for an interview, go NOW and buy one that fits the description of the perfect suit on page 73. Review **Ace the Interview** on page 128 and the **"Just the Basics: A Quick Reference" list** on page 168. Make sure you take a copy with you to the store so you can purchase the perfect shirt and tie as well.

Beyond the Basics

My Associates and I have had hundreds of calls through the years from firms and organizations who want our assistance in upgrading/updating the image of one of their employees whom they are "grooming" (obviously in more ways than one) to move "up." One was for the president of a successful small company who was going to have to start making sales presentations to a giant company. Another was a U.S. senator, and yet another from a multinational company that wanted to send one of their vice presidents overseas to head up one of their offices in Europe. All of these individuals knew their "stuff"—they just didn't **look** like they knew what they were doing. How much faster would they have risen through the ranks if they had "looked the part" earlier in their careers?

Looking the part for any given industry is made up of a series of small but significant details. If you are feeling a bit apprehensive, don't give up. Just like a mountain of work becomes manageable when you tackle one thing at a time, understanding the "details" allows you to start *dressing smart* from your first purchase—from your first day on the job, for the rest of your life.

Follow the Rules to the Top

Just the Basics

- ♣ Look appropriate and great every day.

- ♣ Look elegant, and behave in an elegant manner.

- ♣ Follow any dress code rules, spoken or unspoken, until you get to make the rules—even if they seem foolish.

- ♣ In order to successfully break a rule, you have to **know** the rule.

Beyond the Basics

Some businesses don't have a dress code and others have gotten so casual that "business casual" means that you can wear anything you want—right? For someone else, yes. For **you**, not exactly. No matter how casually you are *allowed* to dress, there are three "rules" that you will want to make for yourself.

Rule #1
Make it a point to *always look great*.

Whether you are wearing classic business, business casual, or strictly casual attire, you will look *equally* appropriate and pulled together!

When you read the words *always look great*, did you just think, "Now I have to be rich and look just like I stepped out of *GQ*, too?" You don't have to be a trend maker, clothes buff, or have a lot of money to look great every day!

Great looking, accomplished men come in all shapes, sizes, and ages. They may be on a tight budget, affluent, or somewhere between. They may be shy, outgoing, or both, depending on the circumstances. Although they may spend very little, or a lot, on their clothes, they do have one thing in common—they all have *developed* a *look*—they have **style** and **elegance!** It's not about dressing "up"—these men even look great in their workout clothes.

Rule #2
Always look *elegant* and behave in an *elegant* manner.

Just what does the word *elegant* mean? Lots of things, all good, including:

- Behaving nicely toward others—being gracious.
- Moving well instead of stomping or clomping.
- Sounding elegant—both the tone of your voice and the words you choose to say.
- Having a "pulled-together look."
- Having charm and good social skills.
- Not wearing your trousers or your tie too short.
- Having clean hair, polished shoes, and a pleasant scent.
- Never making someone feel inelegant, awkward, or less—arrogance does not wear well.
- Dressing and behaving appropriately for your place of business and the occasion—A CLASS ACT!

You work on being gracious and charming (*attitude),* and we'll work together on the rest. One thing you will find is that as your self-assurance gets stronger, you will automatically feel and act more charming and gracious.

Rule #3
Always look *smart*, act *smart,* and be *smart*.

This means, among other things, playing by any dress code "rules" your workplace or industry has (written or understood) until you get to the top, at which time **YOU** get to set the standard—I know it will be a classy one.

Create a look for yourself that is even more *businesslike* than the code suggests. Look totally elegant and pulled together every day and avoid creating any "visual barrier" that may keep you from reaching your career goals.

Wearing clothing viewed as appropriate for your workplace gives the impression that you are highly competent and a team player—it can make you appear to have more knowledge and know-how than others. Be aware that you do need to know your "stuff," too.

Dress equal to, or better than, the top man in your company. Does that mean that you have to dress up every day when everyone else gets to be more casual? If you want an edge, an advantage, you will happily dress, not necessarily up, but "better" than you need to. It may be as simple as wearing a jacket when everyone else is in shirt sleeves or wearing a *nice* long-sleeved shirt with nice trousers when others are in jeans and T-shirts. Think *quality,* not quantity. Elegant simplicity, not overdone. Never be afraid to wear the same *smart* look often.

Dressing smart also means looking the "part" EVERY DAY, no exceptions. It's what you'll want to do if you want to get a job, keep your job, get a promotion, and maybe even connect with that woman you keep noticing who works on the 6th floor.

ACCIDENTALLY LOOKING GREAT

JUST THE BASICS

- If you don't look terrific every day, it means that on the day you did look great it was an accident. Because you don't know how to achieve this look *consistently*, it shows that you don't know how you did it—it was a fluke.

- Don't disappoint—it causes doubt.

BEYOND THE BASICS

Is the way you look that important? In a restaurant if the server is sloppy, surely the food is bad or the kitchen is dirty. If you walked into a store (any store) that appeared messy and ill kept, you would probably think the merchandise was of low quality. The least this negative image would do is cast a doubt in your mind. *Don't give any person room for doubt.* It's so easy to create the right image and it takes so long to erase even one bad impression.

Although it happens every day, it's hard to give you a real-life "business example" of what can happen to you when you don't *dress smart* because guys don't generally go around saying, "Gosh, I got passed over for a promotion because I don't look like I could handle the job."

On the other hand, I do hear tons of stories about women rejecting men because of the way they dress. A pretty friend enjoyed chatting on an airplane with a nice looking lawyer wearing a lawyer-like dark suit. She found him fun and interesting and hoped he would ask for her number. He did. When they got up out of their seats to leave the airplane, he suddenly plopped a wrinkled olive green floppy canvas hat on his head that had little fishing lures dangling all over it. Talk about "instant impact"—he looked so goofy that when he called to ask her out she pretended to have just found her soul mate—somebody else. He made a superb first impression, but she couldn't get past the second. Shallow behavior on her part? Maybe. But once "turned off," it's hard to change a mind.

Here's one example of what can happen when you "look the part." A special friend who was selling high-end real estate (he was in his 20s at the time) volunteered to help out whenever a U.S. vice president traveled to the area of the country where he lived. My friend so impressed this vice president that when he became president, he invited him to move to Washington and join the White House staff. While at the White House, he met and impressed other "important" people and ended up running a multi-billion dollar company. Of course my friend is *smart*—and smart enough to take my advice about his wardrobe!

All it takes to consistently look great is:

◆ Becoming aware.

◆ Gaining knowledge.

◆ Training your eye.

◆ Applying this knowledge and your trained eye to your specific career and lifestyle.

◆ The willingness to put your new knowledge into daily practice.

◆ Maintaining your sense of humor.

Just because you think nothing important is happening "that" day, always dress as if it will—yes, **always**. One phone call or chance meeting can change your life—forever, or not—your choice. If the boss took a quick look around the room because he or she needed someone who could be trusted to go IMMEDIATELY to the executive offices for whatever reason, would you look the part?

Get in the habit of always looking great. It doesn't take any more time, effort, or money, once you have it down pat. In the beginning, time and money are invested to find/buy what you need. Then, all you have to do is combine and wear what you have—*easy elegance*.

 ## EFFECTIVE PACKAGING—NEVER FEAR SHOWING YOUR BEST SIDE

JUST THE BASICS

📦 Don't be afraid to be noticed—if you want to move up, this is the one thing, other than good technical skills and people skills, that you'll need.

BEYOND THE BASICS

Let's say that you have been going to work looking *less than fabulous.* What are "people" going to say when they notice (and they will) that you look different? Heaven forbid that you might turn heads when you walk into a room or into a meeting. In order to continue to accomplish your work in an exceptional way, you have no reason to revert to looking unexceptional. Only a jealous person would prefer that you look forgettable.

Don't be fearful that you will look "overdone" and that people will be scrutinizing you with raised eyebrows instead of admiration. *Easy elegance* is never flashy or too complicated. Your look will be totally understated, yet classy. As you continue to train your eye and put your knowledge into practice, you will put any fears to rest.

LOOK *SMART*—BUY *SMART*

JUST THE BASICS

◆ If it isn't *equal to or better than* the best look you have right now, leave it.

◆ Spend the most money on clothes you spend the most time in.

BEYOND THE BASICS

If you truly want to continually upgrade your look, you'll want to always apply this *smart tip* so when you shop you won't be just fattening your closet. It's much more difficult to have a lot of bad choices—that's one of the reasons you will hear women who have a closet full of clothes say, "I have nothing to wear!" It can be confusing and what they are really saying is that they don't have anything that they like that is appropriate for what they want to do. It is far better to wear the same outstanding look once or twice a week than to wear something else that looks "so-so" on you.

> Buy well the first time—well made, well cut, wonderful classic clothes won't go out of style. — JoAnna

For most men today, money and time are a huge investment. If what you buy "sets you back" instead of moves you forward, it doesn't make sense. Don't spend money on something that doesn't flatter you. You can't afford to look great one day and not the next. It can give the impression that you don't know what you're doing. People who can be consistently counted on are the ones who are promoted—your visual presentation is as important as a work presentation. It doesn't sound fair, but that's the way it often works.

Clothing is an investment in your future, but it's NOT a good investment if it doesn't look like "a million dollars" on you.

WEAR BOARDROOM LOOKS
INSTEAD OF BACKROOM LOOKS

JUST THE BASICS

- ♣ Look like a potential leader instead of a worker bee.

- ♣ Invest in your future.

BEYOND THE BASICS

If you have a commanding presence, everyone will expect that you are a
leader—even if you are just starting out. How many boardroom looks do
you have? How many do you need to have? How many suits and jackets do
you have that you only wear when you think nothing important is going to
happen that day?

? ? Questions, questions, and more questions. Who did I write this
book for? Executives, management, entry level? It's for **every** man who
wants to look his best. And it's for any man who has sat at the same
desk for more than a year or two when he wants to move up; the man
who knows as much or more than his boss, but he isn't one. Perhaps
you've met the head man several times, but he doesn't remember you;
you don't feel confident, or you don't appear confident. I want you to look
so pulled together every day that when someone new walks into your
office or sees you at a meeting, they will think **you** are the boss.

When you are shopping for new clothes, you want to be able to look in
the mirror and say, "Yes, I look and feel like a million dollars." If you can't say
it, leave it—you will find something perfect in another aisle or another store.
Million-dollar looks have nothing to do with how much money you spend on
your clothing, but they do have everything to do with investment—*a lifetime
investment*—because your future will be much brighter based on the way
you look right now.

**You don't have to spend any additional money on clothing and
accessories that will give you the look you want**, but you may have
to invest a little more time to find quality clothing at bargain prices. If
you are not on a strict budget and/or don't have the time or the patience to shop, go directly to the men's wear department of quality
stores. The advice and tailoring will most often be excellent, with, perhaps, the exception of advice on color. **You** will want to be in charge of
what colors and color combinations you wear—it will be worth it. More
about that later. When the compliments start coming in, you'll feel more
confident. You will carry yourself differently—even sit differently in meetings (and on dates).

BE CAREFUL NOT TO GET TOO *CASUAL*— THINK BIG PICTURE

JUST THE BASICS

◆ Dressing too casually is a mistake.

◆ Dress better than you have to.

◆ Dress as well as the top men in your company.

BEYOND THE BASICS

If you are dressed too casually for *your* workplace, you are making the visual statement that you don't know what's appropriate and/or that you don't care.

Some examples of styles and garments that are not correct for business casual at some firms but appropriate for others are: jeans, sweatshirts, rugby shirts, athletic footwear, deck shoes, any shoes without socks, and T-shirts.

While none of these are acceptable business casual in a conservative law firm, each are allowed in some place of business: a sports magazine editor wearing jeans and a T-shirt with a good-looking odd jacket; a man who sells boats wearing deck shoes without socks, and a football coach in a rugby shirt.

You are always making visual statements. No matter where you are going or what you are doing, you are telling people something about yourself. Thinking "big picture" means that to get where you want to be in three years, for example, you may have to pay extra close attention to those visual statements you are making today.

DON'T SACRIFICE COMFORT FOR LOOKS OR LOOKS FOR COMFORT

JUST THE BASICS

◆ Comfort and sloppy are not synonyms.

◆ Wearing something that hurts, binds, or itches is not smart.

◆ You can have both style and comfort if you practice *smart tips* and a little restraint.

BEYOND THE BASICS

Sloppy equals incompetence in the minds of many people. A sloppy appearance, created by poorly put-together, ill-fitting, unwashed, unironed, mismatched, or stretched-out clothing, sends the message that you don't care how you look and that "you don't have a clue." It makes a *loud* statement that you are not confident or competent in *at least one* aspect of your life—perhaps casting doubt on your competence in other areas.

On the other hand, comfort, grubby, baggy, and sloppy are not synonyms. Since comfort can be found in any style and shape, it's never necessary to make this sacrifice. When you try something on, sit in it, walk around in it, and ask yourself how it feels on your body. Confining? Scratchy? Uncomfortably tight when you sit? Will you happily reach for it all of the time? Is one size larger the answer?

Most every day in your place of work someone, maybe you, has sacrificed comfort for style. You got a terrific bargain on a suit, but it reminds you of your itchy trousers when you were a boy. Even though your great-looking new shoes hurt when you tried them on, you bought them anyway because the salesperson assured you that your feet would stretch them. Clothing and accessories that annoy or cause discomfort start getting left in your closet, making you feel guilty (and less smart) because you wasted your money on them.

Follow the *smart tip*—don't buy it unless it is *equal to, or more comfortable than the best look you have right now*. And, carefully remove all scratchy tags before you wear something for the first time. If you don't, you may be tempted to rip it out in the middle of the day. The annoyance factor can contaminate the way you feel about the item, keeping you from wanting to wear it again.

DEFINING STYLE:

ALWAYS READ THE SMALL PRINT

JUST THE BASICS

 Develop a sense of style that will work for you, not against you.

 Whatever your job, look like you are the one who can be trusted to get it done right.

BEYOND THE BASICS

ALL of the *smart tips* in this book will help you develop a stylish, yet businesslike look uniquely your own. Each tip you put into practice will bring you closer to training your eye to see what works for you and what doesn't.

You'll look in the mirror and be able to say, "This suit looks drab on me. I need more of a solid color, not a blended look." "This jacket is styled slightly longer than a classic jacket, but I like it for a change." "To keep the proportion right for me, the trousers will need to be tapered to make them slightly narrower so it doesn't look like I'm wearing a *tall* when I should be wearing a *regular*." Trust me, you will be able to tell—just put yourself in my classroom until the end of the book and then put your new knowledge to work for you.

Style—it even sounds like a *smart* word but what does it mean? It's a word that has a myriad of meanings, all directly related to what you want to achieve.

   One connotation is something you strive for, *being stylish,* as in looking fashionable, contemporary, sophisticated, and pulled together.

   Another has to do with **the** *shape* or *line* **of a garment**—there are many styles of jackets and trousers. Jacket styles range from single-breasted 1-button to 4- to-5-button (with the classics being the 2- and 3-button). Double-breasted styles range from the classic 6-button to the fashion designers' desire to do things differently—the 2-button, 4-button, and 8-button. Even within the classics there are differences in styling, including the number of vents. Trouser styles vary from flat front to 1 pleat, 2 pleats, and 3 pleats.

   Finally, the word *style* **can refer to a** *specific style* **of dress**—western, funky, faddish, trendy, up-fashion, casual, business casual, classic business, conservative business, formal, sporty, arty, vintage, and eccentric.

   I met with a woman one day who wanted so much for her husband to dress the way he used to—in classic elegant attire. She wanted him to have a consultation with me in hopes that I could get him to change back. As the story goes, he took a trip—I think it was to Wichita—and when he came back, he decided to dress only in western attire—western-styled jackets, shirts with snaps, cowboy boots, and ties with a western motif. He rode horses daily and had for years before. His occupation? Owner of a major construction company. Lifestyle? Grand. Region of country? Major metropolitan east coast.

   We met and talked—he knew of his wife's wishes. I asked him if he wanted to consider giving up his western attire. He said never. I gave him some ideas how he could look great every day, regardless of day or evening, business or social events. He was willing to wear a classic tuxedo to formal affairs but not a classic dark suit to dressy evening affairs. Money was not an object.

   This is what we/I did: He had been ordering his western jackets out of catalogs—average cost, $99. We met with the finest tailor in town and he made a beautiful navy blue western jacket (piping and all) and matching trousers out of the best fabric available. At a dressy evening function, at a glance you wouldn't have noticed the styling, only a very well dressed man.

   I met with the man who used to make this gentleman's classic dress shirts and picked out wonderful fabrics, solid colors, and classic western checks, color-perfect for my client, to be made into western-style shirts with snaps. I telephoned Neiman Marcus in Dallas and Houston and found super everyday jackets in several colors—western in styling, of course. I bought color-coordinating ties from Hermes (his personal favorite brand) in western motifs.

   I coordinated his new looks with the best of his old and made him a journal so he wouldn't have to remember all of his new combinations. Was his wife happy? Much happier because he once again looked fabulous every day. Could I have accomplished this on a budget? Absolutely.

If it complemented your career goals and your personality, you could dress in any style you wanted or even a different style every day if you like—having no set style is a style of its own.

As a young woman, I was told that I should find my own style and stick with it. What I found was that I like several different styles, depending on how I feel, where I am going, who I am going with, and what I want to accomplish once I get there.

It only makes sense for me to dress differently for a meeting with the chairman of a conservative corporation who wants to talk about the services my company can provide than I do if I am going to lunch with a newspaper fashion editor. Of course, I dress even differently yet when meeting *potential* future mothers-in-law than when I'm presenting a seminar in Paris at the invitation of the American Embassy, going to a state dinner at the White House in honor of a king and queen, or heading into the jungle to go down the headwaters of the Amazon.

Can you wear more contemporary business looks when you are a man of a certain age? Of course, but I suppose I should be more *specific* for those of you who might be concerned. First we should define what that age is—but we can't, because, it's not an age exactly—it is any time at which you would look ridiculous in what you are wearing. Before you get dressed in the morning, ask yourself the following: Where are you going? Who are you going with? What are you trying to accomplish there? What impression do you want others to have of you?

In other words, what image will best serve your needs at any given time? When you are going to a meeting with your boss, he needs to be proud to be seen with you and, for both of your sakes, you need to look like you know what you are doing—no doubt. What image do you need if you are meeting/calling on clients who wear jeans and T-shirts, or uniforms, for a living? What if you are from a big city and they live in a small town in the middle of what you might think of as nowhere ?

Consider the **trust factor**. Clients need to trust that you are giving them good advice (selling them what they need, for example) and your image can exude trust, or doubt. They also need to feel that you are just enough like them that you understand their business—so they can relate to you—you have common ground. All this boils down to the fact that you can't dress like them. You *have* to look like an expert in your field because an expert, not a neighbor or best friend, is what they need and want. — JoAnna

DRESSING SMART FOR *YOUR* INDUSTRY

JUST THE BASICS

- ▲ Look *better* than you are expected to look—*equal to or better than* the top guy.

BEYOND THE BASICS

How are the top-level men in your industry expected to dress—totally classic, conservative, more up-fashion, trendy, casual, or business casual? Once you identify the *required* look of your work realm, you can plan a wardrobe based on this expected attire. Why should you? To disappoint with your image can keep you from moving up. Straying too far from the expected could get you noticed—noticed in a positive or negative way, depending on which direction you stray.

For each field, there will be regional differences and differences even within regions, sometimes due to climate, "cultures," and big city/small town influences. There will also be differences even within the same city. In Washington, DC, for example, one would think that our government agencies would follow a specific dress code. But, no, each has different policies on what employees can wear to work.

> Once when I was presenting a wardrobe seminar to the Congressional Wives Club I had the nerve to tell them how extra important it was that they look great every day. No excuses. Why? Because everywhere they went, they represented **me** and every other American woman.
>
> I explained that in this country, women look at them and say, "Oh, that's the wife of Congressman so and so—look at what she's wearing." When traveling in foreign countries, the local women say (pretend that this is written in French or Italian), "Look, that's Senator so and so's wife—that must be how American women are dressing now."

Whatever you do for a living, you will want to *look smart* but this is one area where you will want to **think smart**, as well. Play by the rules until you are able to take the lead. Playing by the rules does not mean that I advocate looking bedraggled, drab, or overly conservative just because top men in your field or place of business look this way. I do want you to stand out—in the best possible light.

An example: If you work in a very conservative industry, and you work for one of the most conservative firms, where no man has ever worn a 6-button double-breasted jacket designed to only fasten the bottom button, sometimes referred to as a 6-to-1 (you can substitute your own example), I wouldn't advise that you do, either. As soon as another man in the firm, higher up than you, wears the first 6-to-1, you can *consider* the option. Listen for flack or any negative comments from top leaders. If you think it's safe, go for it in the most professional way—wear one in navy or gray with a white or soft white shirt and a classic, well coordinated tie that is *equal to or better than....*

If you are in one of the conservative fields such as investment banking or law, you will most likely be dressing in classic business attire—*please* don't read boring, mundane, dowdy, or uninteresting into the word "classic." Classic clothing is never really out of style. How *contemporary* classically styled clothing appears is almost always dependent on the cut or design of the garments, classic with a twist, and the way you choose to combine them.

If your industry is strictly business casual or casual, understand really, really well that casual and sloppy, stretched-out, faded-out, and worn-out are not synonyms. Dress with *a studied* casualness (think casual, *easy elegance*) that gives you a well pulled together look. How? You will know exactly how when you start using these *smart tips* and training your eye.

CRACKING THE RIGHT CODE

JUST THE BASICS

- ◆ Dress more businesslike than you are required to.

- ◆ Respect tradition and be true to your own personality and sense of style at the same time.

BEYOND THE BASICS

What do companies do when an employee's image is hurting their business? It's a touchy matter, of course, because they cannot use your appearance as a reason to let you go, but it's very clear that if you don't look the part, they will find a (legal) way to get rid of you. An employee of one of the largest hotel chains in the world wasn't wearing a tie when he called on a client. The client called the chairman of this company and said, "How dare he come to see me without a tie." Yes, how you present yourself is very important—to your job and to your company.

The idea behind business casual was that employees would be happier and therefore more productive. What happened was that not having to wear their familiar uniform and not being allowed to wear their jeans, men got stressed out because they felt they needed a different wardrobe—one that they didn't know how to put together. Part of the problem is that there is a huge leeway between suits and ties and denim, and many men chose attire too close to the casual end of the spectrum.

Examples of Dress Codes

The GAO (Government Accounting Office), an agency that one would think of as conservative, has a formal policy of 24/7 business casual all year (it started as Fridays, progressed to all summer, then went to all year). *But*, their policy also states that you have to dress for business if you have an outside meeting or if people are coming in from the outside to meet with you.

In the hospitality industry some high-end hotels often have strict guidelines, uniform-like dark suits, or furnished uniforms, for front desk personnel or anyone who might be interacting with clients. Even in the office at the Ritz Carlton hotels, for example, the dress code is suit and tie. On the other hand, at the Marriott hotels the guidelines are 24/7 business casual, including the front desk.

I spoke with a senior partner in a typical Washington law firm where, although the dress code is business casual 24/7, the lawyers are counseled to "dress for their day," meaning that if they have a client meeting they should assume that the client will be in suit and tie and, therefore, so should they. When they first instigated this code, everyone took full advantage of it. Now, the dress seems to be divided by age. The older men are wearing suits/jackets and ties, and the younger men are more casual. Would you like to guess which group most of the partners fall in? With the trend moving toward more formal business attire, it's likely that this firm will soon require suit and tie on Monday through Thursday.

Although it's important to always *feel* appropriate, business dress doesn't always mean coat and tie. At the Industrial Credit Union in Bellingham, Washington, business dress is required Monday through Thursday, and Friday is business casual.

Their business dress policy shows suit or jacket and tie as optional and the only thing in the required column is socks. The never column is as follows: Athletic socks, baseball caps, both long- and short-sleeve sport shirts, denim, polo/golf shirts (knit shirts), flannel shirts, sweatshirts, T-shirts, tank tops, jeans (any color), sweat pants or warm-ups (any style), shorts (walking or Bermuda), leather topsider style shoes, boots (cowboy or hiking), canvas shoes, tennis shoes (any type), running shoes, and sandals/thongs.

For Friday business casual, approved ICU shirts and sweaters are required (they have the credit union's logo on them), jeans are allowed, as are tennis shoes, topsiders, cowboy boots, and hiking boots—Bellingham is on the northwest coast, about 15 minutes from the Canadian border. Socks are still required and the only things on the never list are athletic socks, baseball caps, sweat pants or warm-ups, shorts, and sandals/thongs.

To gather the "best of the best" information for this book, I interviewed many men who are experts in the field of dressing men, including a former president of Brooks Brothers.

One of my experts recently attended a seminar for CEOs where the literature said that business casual was the appropriate dress for the gathering. Seventy-five percent of the men showed up in suit and tie—including him. He just doesn't feel comfortable doing business in casual clothes.

Sometimes it comes down to a matter of respect—respect of tradition, respect of others, respect of self. President Bush is a casual kind of guy on his ranch in Texas, but he will not enter the Oval Office without putting on a tie—neither will anyone else who works at the White House. When you understand the "rules," you will know when you can ignore them—

I'm sure that in a national emergency the president and his staff would not stop to put on a tie before entering the Oval Office.

Color Power

It's Your Most Important Accessory
and It is Free

Just the Basics

Use color to give yourself an edge.

Beyond the Basics

Why am I calling color an accessory? Because it is an *adornment.* If you know how to use colors complimentary to your coloring, you will look more phenomenal, by far, than you can without this knowledge. Edith Head, the famous Hollywood costume designer, referred to color as a *powerful tool* that should be used as a precision instrument.

Color has an amazing impact. According to research done by the Wharton School of Business and the University of Minnesota, color accelerates learning retention and recall by 55% to 78%; it improves and increases comprehension up to 73%; increases willingness to read up to 80%; and sells products and ideas more effectively by 50% to 85%. The Beach Boys, former clients of mine, wanted to know what their best colors would be for both their *signature statement* Hawaiian shirts and the backdrops for their stage sets. The result was that not only did they look great individually, they looked like a band, instead of just several individuals doing their own thing.

Let me tell you right now that I do not believe in any of the seasonal or cool/warm color theories. This is what I *do* believe: Approximately 50% of you look fabulous in bright, clear, vibrant colors. The other half of you look exceptional in colors that have less brightness—those that are more subdued or muted looking.

Do You Look Essential ⭐
Or Insignificant? ⭐

Just the Basics

★ If you wear colors that are too toned down for your coloring, you will look insignificant.

★ If you wear colors that are too bright for your coloring, you could look ill.

BEYOND THE BASICS

What is *clarity*? Clarity has to do with the amount of "brightness," or lack of brightness, of a color—how "clear" or "toned down" the color appears. *ALL* colors (red, blue, green, and so on) come in different clarities—from very bright to very toned down.

Picture the brightest red you have ever seen. Maybe it's fire engine red. Now picture a toned down, quieter version of the same red.

Very bright, clear colors, like fire engine red, lack brown or gray pigments. Toned down colors are clear colors that have been softened/muted with gray or brown pigment. The more gray or brown pigment that is added, the more toned down the color becomes. There are:

☆ Bright, bold, vivid, brilliant, intense, vibrant, clear colors.

☆ Dazzling, radiant, lively, clear colors that are bright, but more "subtle" looking (not as bold or intense) as those above.

☆ Gutsy, but not bright, rich, muted, burnished, spicy, slightly toned down colors.

☆ Restrained, reserved, calm, quiet colors, that are more subdued, less gutsy, than those just above.

Don't be fooled by advice that muted, subdued tones are always elegant—they are only elegant for half of you, and the other half of you will just look insignificant if you wear them.

If a color is **too** bright or bold for your coloring, it can appear garish, and, by comparison, you will look washed-out and overly pale, even sickly. That's a clue that you are one of those men who will be more enhanced by subtle looking brights or by more subdued, muted, toned down colors.

If, on the other hand, a color is **too** subdued or toned down for your coloring, it can gray, muddy, or even sallow your skin, causing you to look drab. That's your clue that you are in the approximately 50% of men who are more enhanced by bright and bold, or bright but subtle, clear, vibrant colors.

You can experiment in front of a mirror—it's very important to use good light. Hold different clarities up to your face. Work with any colors you like. If you don't have many colors around, do this in a store (don't pay any attention to raised eyebrows—you are training your eye and you will *live* through this experiment). Start with a comparison of bright colors—one **BOLD** and bright, the other **more subtle** yet still vibrant and bright. Holding up the boldest, brightest first, glance at yourself and see if your eye goes right to the color or whether it goes to your face and the color at the same time. What you are looking for is a good "fit" for your skin tone and hair color.

If you **hold your own** and your face looks fresh, radiant, and alive, the boldest, brightest colors will look outstanding on you. If your glance brings your eyes immediately to the color, this clarity is too bright and bold for your coloring.

Try a more subtle looking bright color next. If your face lights up and looks clear and healthy, you've found your best clarity. But, if the color still appears to jump forward or jump off your skin, and you look washed-out, pale, or sickly, you'll know that you need yet more subdued, toned down colors to make **YOU** look your best.

If you compare just slightly toned down, subdued colors to very toned down, subdued colors, you will find that you look more healthy in one or the other of these clarities. Watch for your face to "light up" versus appearing dulled or grayed. The right clarity brightens your face, making it appear healthy and alive, while the wrong clarity instantly dulls your skin (like a shadow has been cast upon it), taking away your healthy look.

Look Distinguished—Not Drab

Just the Basics

♦ You can successfully wear at least one shade of every color in the spectrum.

♦ If you are going to wear a red tie, for example, make sure that the shade of red you choose looks wonderful on **you**, rather than on somebody else.

Beyond the Basics

Now that you have an understanding about the importance of clarity, we need to work on *shade*. There are many different shades of every color in the spectrum and you'll look extraordinary in **your** shade of blue and **your** gray, for example, but not so "hot" in your best friend's blue or gray— remember that you will be wearing your best shades (of every color) in your best *clarity*.

Let's take gray as an example, for whether you are wearing a gray business suit or a gray sweater, you want a shade of gray that enhances your appearance. Grays come in a variety of shades from those that look brownish to those that are bluish-gray in tone. You will **not** be equally flattered by all grays.

Every one of you can wear at least one **specific shade** of *every color* in the spectrum and look outstanding—on some of you, a few of your best shades may need to be combined or accented with another, to create the right strength or subtleness for you. There are **numerous** different shades of:

♦ white ("white" is flattering to all, but *pure* white is a different story)

♦ beige   ♦ camel   ♦ brown

- gray
- green
- blue-green
- robin's egg blue/teal
- blue
- purple
- plum/fuchsia
- raspberry
- red
- red-coral
- coral
- orange
- yellow and gold
- rust
- navy
- black (most, but not all, men can wear black effectively in some way)

I know that some of you have just decided that I'm crazy because I'm telling you that you can wear a color that **you're certain** you don't look good in—green, yellow, or brown, perhaps. Actually, if you haven't been wearing these colors, I'm delighted, because if you don't know exactly which *shade* of each of these looks great on you, it's easy to make a **MAJOR** mistake—one that can muddy, gray or yellow your skin.

Of all of the greens, for instance, lime, celery, Kelly, mint, olive, jade, parrot, spring, emerald, sea, forest, apple, moss, sage, and grass, there is most often only **one** that will be super on you. Yellow can be difficult, but when you get it right, it's terrific. Brown may be the hardest to get right, because if you don't get it **perfect**, it can be a disaster as a clothing color. But when it's good, it's very, very good.

🚫 **Bad Advice:** To find out if you're cool or warm, hold rasp-berries up to your face. If you look good, you're cool and you should wear only cool colors. Or, if you look better when you hold tomatoes up, you are *warm*—having nothing to do with how much charm you might have.

☾ **My Advice:** You may be a *cool cat* or a hot, oh, I'm sorry, *warm-blooded* male, but when it comes to colors, everyone can wear both "cool" and "warm."

Without seeing you in person, it's difficult to guide you to your very best *shades*. Like wearing the wrong clarity, the wrong shade of a color can cause you to look drab or ill. It's **equally** important that you learn to recognize the shades and clarities of colors that give you a healthy, suc-cessful appearance.

Do women instinctively know what colors are flattering to them? Rarely. What most women do when they look in the mirror is to check out everything from the neck down—the style and the fit. Just like most men, because their eye hasn't been trained to see what the color is do-ing to their skin tone, they seldom are accurate when it comes to choos-ing their best colors. Guys also usually just check themselves out from the neck down.

> Your favorite colors may not have anything to do with what looks
> good on you. — JoAnna

COLORING WITHIN THE LINES

JUST THE BASICS

◆ Add variety to your shirt, sweater, and tie wardrobes by wearing more color.

BEYOND THE BASICS

Many of you are color shy, except for blue. The fastest way to give variety to your suits and jackets and trousers is to add color. Here are some *colorful smart tips* for those of you who want to give it a chance:

◆ **The most wearable shades of green** have a touch of blue in them (like emerald green), versus the more yellow greens (such as lime green).

◆ **Blue-greens, turquoises, robin's egg blue, and teal are universally flattering colors**—don't forget to wear them in your best clarity.

◆ **A blue shirt is just not a blue shirt.** There are many shades of blue that have a slight purplish cast and they are not as universally enhancing as more true blues. It's actually easy to see—just hold a couple of different looking blue shirts side by side.

◆ **Every one of you can wear several shades of purple**—remember your best clarity, as more grayed down purples can look very drab in dim lighting conditions.

◆ **Each of you can wear a shade of raspberry.** In the case of plum and fuchsia, you can find a becoming shade, but be very careful here—the wrong shade can really sallow your skin.

◆ **You all have your best red**—your body's natural red color is a deeper tone of the color you naturally "blush." You can see the lighter version of your red, your pink, in your finger tips and the inside of your lower lip.

◆ **All of you can wear a shade of coral**, and you can also wear a shade of red-coral—picture a shade that would fall right between your best red and your coral.

- ◆ **Orange is available to all of you,** but the shade of orange that you may be *picturing* is wearable by only a few of you. The most flattering oranges have pink in them and are often very close in shade to your coral.

- ◆ **Everyone can wear at least one shade of yellow**—when you picture how many different shades of yellow there are, that will help you understand that someplace between buttercup and lemon, there will be a shade that is perfect for you. Beware of the more brownish golden yellows like mustard, because they will muddy, gray, green, or sallow your skin.

- ◆ **What about gold?** Not everyone can wear a shade of gold successfully. If you don't look equally as good in a gold as you do in your yellow, avoid it. If you *love* gold and want to wear it anyway, wear it with other enhancing colors or mixed in a print of a tie.

USING NEUTRALS TO LOOK ASTUTE,

NOT AUSTERE

JUST THE BASICS

Just because it's a neutral color doesn't mean it's *safe* or will be flattering to you.

BEYOND THE BASICS

The guidelines below will help you select the best shades of neutrals for your coloring:

Your best beige matches your skin tone exactly or, if your skin is darker, it is a lighter version of your exact skin tone.

If your hair is light, your best camels will match your hair, hair highlight, or be a darker version of it. **Your best brown** will be a darker version of your hair color and/or your hair highlight color.

If your hair is a medium brown, your best camels will be your skin tone, a darker version of your skin tone, or possibly a lighter version of your hair color and/or hair highlight color. **Your best browns** will be a darker version of your hair color and/or your hair highlight color.

If your hair is brown, your best camel will be a darker version of your skin tone or match your skin tone; if your skin tone is darker, a lighter version of your skin tone or, possibly, your hair highlight color. **Your best browns** will match your hair color and/or hair highlight color.

&⌢ **If your hair is very, very dark brown or black, your best camel** will either be a darker or lighter version of your skin tone or will match it exactly. **Your best browns** will be a darker version of your skin tone, or, if your skin tone is darker, they will match it exactly. With very, very dark brown hair, black is often the better choice when it comes to clothing color.

&⌢ **Your best gray** will not have any brownish or muddy quality to it— more pure grays and blue-grays are more universally enhancing. **Charcoal gray** is an outstanding color for suits and a good option to black for those of you who find that black isn't flattering or that it is too heavy looking or too formal for you.

&⌢ **Your best rust** will not look burgundy, orangish, or brownish on you—it will look "rust."

&⌢ **You may be able to wear several shades of navy,** but they will all have something in common—they will be lighter or darker versions of the same *shade* of navy, which is very handy when you want to combine them. Avoid shades of navy that sallow or gray your skin.

&⌢ **Other dark neutrals**—forest green (varying shades of dark green) works best for those of you who are enhanced by slightly toned down or toned down colors; drab burgundy that is brownish look- ing, unlike the color you see when light shines through a glass of red wine, is rarely flattering to anyone. Burgundy and olive were the most over-rated colors of the last century.

&⌢ You'll be learning all about your best **whites** soon.

Black—does it look sophisticated or deadly on you? Most, but not all, of you can wear black and look fabulous. For those of you who can wear black well, head-to-toe black will be flattering to some, but for others it's *how* you wear it can make the difference between looking elegant or drab. On some of you, black will need:

&⌢ A touch of color near the face—shirt under a black jacket.

&⌢ More skin showing—black V-neck versus turtleneck.

&⌢ Less black—just shoes and a belt instead of a suit.

&⌢ To be combined with your skin tone and/or hair colors—a hair color or skin tone jacket (brown, camel/caramel, bronze, beige) over black trousers and a black shirt. "Tying" the black into your skin tone and hair color creates balance and makes it look like there is a *relation-ship* between your coloring and the black.

℞ To be used sparingly—only a small amount of black in a print combined with your best colors and neutrals, or don't wear it at all.

How can you tell which is your most flattering way(s) to wear black? You are going to be training your eye, and your mirror will help you figure it out. Experiment with the various ways listed above. If you find that, no matter what you do, black looks out of place or "foreign" on you, avoid wearing it except perhaps as shoes and a belt when necessary.

ESSENTIAL ACCENTS

JUST THE BASICS

É   If you look washed-out, try adding a color accent near your face.

É   Know what colors to avoid in general.

BEYOND THE BASICS

There are some colors that just work best when they are accented, near the face, with a touch of another color (sometimes the accent can be one of your best neutrals, as well). Not all of you will need this accent, but here's a list to be suspicious of:

É   beige, tan, and taupe

É   camel and khaki

É   olive

É   brown

É   bronze

É   gray

É   rust

É   navy

É   pastels

É   very dark colors

É   black

Information generally reserved for women, but important for you as well, is that some of the colors listed above may work on you in the daytime without an accent but may require one at night or under presentation lighting. Poor lighting can drain color out of your face, so it's best to avoid wearing an "iffy" look.

Select the Right White Shirt for Your Tie

A "white shirt" does not go well with every tie.

NO **The pure white shirt makes the cream in this tie look dirty.**

YES **A tie with creamy white is best paired with a creamy white shirt.**

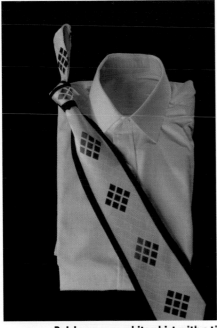

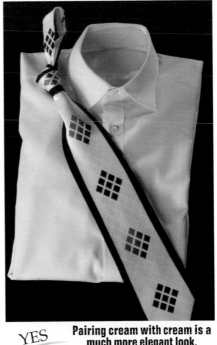

NO **Pairing a pure white shirt with a tie that has creamy white in it makes both look cheap.**

YES **Pairing cream with cream is a much more elegant look.**

Clothing and accessories courtesy of Macy's.
Photos courtesy of The Photographer's Gallery.

Smart Chart for:
Muted Coloring

Smart Chart for:
Contrast Coloring

Smart Chart for:

Light-Bright Coloring

Smart Chart for:

Gentle Coloring

There are many shades of beige, camel, brown, and navy.

Your personal best beiges, camels, and browns will match your skin tone, be a lighter or darker version of your skin tone, and/or match your hair color and hair highlight colors. Wearing your most flattering shades of gray and navy are equally as important as selecting your best shades and clarity of every color. Black is a "possibility" for all color types, but will not be a great head-to-toe look for every individual.

Half of you look great in clear, bright colors, a pure white shirt, and high contrast. The other half of you look great in less bright colors, soft-white and creamy white shirts, and softer contrast.

Softer contrast tie on a creamy white shirt.
YES for Gentle and Muted color types.

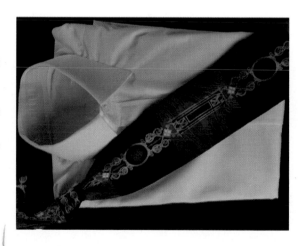

YES Toned-down, less bright colors in tie paired with creamy white shirt.

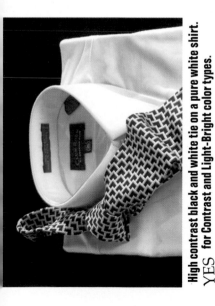

High contrast black and white tie on a pure white shirt.
YES for Contrast and Light-Bright color types.

YES Bright, clear colors in tie paired with pure white shirt.

Selecting the best clarity (brightness of color) and pattern size for your color type can make the difference between a great look or an insignificant look.

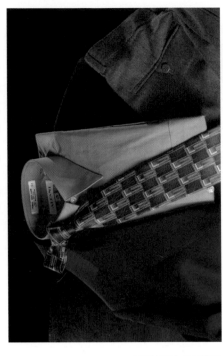

Light-Bright Coloring: Bright, but less bold, medium or small pattern sizes or visually lightweight larger patterns.

Muted Coloring: Toned-down but gutsy colors, strong small patterns, medium patterns, or large blended-looking patterns.

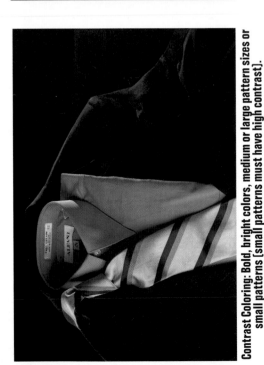

Contrast Coloring: Bold, bright colors, medium or large pattern sizes or small patterns (small patterns must have high contrast).

Gentle Coloring: Toned-down clarity (even less bold), subtle, small or medium sized patterns or blended-looking larger patterns.

What about khaki? The word "khaki" has had several incarnations, and, although it used to be considered the color of "sand," it is now used as a generic term for a fabric finish on casual pants. Khakis can now be found in an entire range of neutrals such as tan, camel, taupe, beige, black, gray, brown, olive green, and navy, as well as sand.

So, when it comes to purchasing khaki trousers in tan, camel, taupe, sand, or beige, for example, buy them in *shades* that work best with your skin tone—believe me, it will never be one of those with an olive or greenish cast. Many years ago olive was dubbed a neutral color when fashion designers decided to make some good-looking styles in this "off" color that tends to muddy, gray, green, or sallow most all skin tones. I've never understood why anyone would want to dress in the color of an olive when there is always a much more flattering choice.

On occasion *GQ Magazine* publishes a list of what every fashionable man should know. One of the things they mentioned you should know was "the colors you can't wear." They didn't list them, but I will give you my list.

Every attempt has been made to match the color combinations of the jackets/trousers/shirts/ties in the photos as closely as possible to that of the actual clothing. We have worked closely with the printer to ensure that the printed charts on the preceding pages match the actual Smart Charts as well. However, as printing runs may differ, there may be slight variations in shades and clarity. To order your own Smart Chart with actual color chips in a convenient pocket size holder go to www.DressingSmart.com or call 202-293-9175. There's a free quiz on the website that will help you figure out your Color Type.

Some colors to avoid in general are:

- ⃠ taupe

- ⃠ putty

- ⃠ oatmeal

- ⃠ olive

- ⃠ muddy or brownish grays

- ⃠ very yellowish greens

- ⃠ oranges the color of pumpkins

- ⃠ mustard

- ⃠ very orangy rusts

⊘   brownish burgundy

If you love wearing a color that doesn't love you, a color-perfect accent near your face in the form of a tie, shirt, or sweater becomes an important layer. Or, since you likely don't spend your day in front of a mirror admiring this color, you could just stop wearing the color and enjoy looking at it on someone else.

Instead of taupe, putty, or oatmeal, wear your best shade of beige. Instead of olive, wear your best shade of camel or your most flattering shades of light and medium brown.

CREATING *INSTANT* IMPACT

JUST THE BASICS

✗   Understanding your unique personal color harmony is an essential key to looking great.

BEYOND THE BASICS

Color is the missing link—everything else can be perfect, but if the color, clarity, or color combination is wrong for YOU, it can cause you to look washed-out, sickly, or ineffective.

Even if a man has a wonderful sense of style, in that he has a knack for creating good looks, if he doesn't pay attention to *his* best colors in *his* best clarity (brightness) AND *his* best color combinations, he may be looking great only from the neck down.

Let's assume that you are wearing your most flattering shades of each color in the spectrum in the best clarity for you. Can you combine these colors in any way you like and look super? Sorry, no. You also have most flattering color combinations.

Why? Half of you have strong coloring and look best in gutsier color combinations. The other half of you have more subtle coloring and look better in less bold color combinations. Once you know your Color Type I'll give you the specifics on *your* best combinations.

What is a Color Type?

A Color Type is simply a *description* of your coloring (skin tone and hair color) and/or a *description* of your best look for clothing (and for a woman, her makeup). For example, if you have ivory, clear olive, clear camel/caramel, or a clear brown skin tone and dark brown or black hair, your best color combinations will have contrast versus being blended looking.

Finding your Color Type

The following lists of men (many of who you may recognize) with their "Color Type," best "clarity," and the designation of strong or subtle will help you make a decision that will be LIFE CHANGING! Why so serious, suddenly? Because, if you want to look your absolute best *FOREVER*, nothing is as important.

Although I have made only four lists, there are really **12** different Color Types because MANY people are a cross between two—half subtle coloring and half strong coloring, for example. If this is you, you will find that you walk a fine line between being overpowered and being under-powered. For some of you, a light just went on—now you know why it has been so hard for you to get it *right*. More about Cross Color Types soon.

⊘ **Bad Advice:** Light hair and skin pairs well with powder blue. Darker complexions look better in bright colors.

① **My Advice:** This is among the worst advice that has been given. How dark or light your skin is has nothing to do with your Color Type—I am referring to all men and especially black men. The darkest skin tones and lightest skin tones are found in all 12 Color Types.

Also, there are no single categories for *all* blonds, *all* brunettes, or *all* redheads, nor are there for **all** Black, Asian, Hispanic, Native American, or Caucasian men. There is a huge variety of coloring among all men, what-ever race. Black, Asian, Native American, Hispanic, and Caucasian men are found in all 12 Color Types. Black and brown hair are in all 12. Natural blonds are in at least 6 different Color Types (could be more—it depends on what you think of as blond), and redheads in 4 (again, depending on what you think of as a redhead).

Your Color Type has nothing to do with your personality, body type, or your eye color—all exist in all 12.

Four Major Color Types

◆ **CONTRAST COLOR TYPES—Bright, Bold Clear Colors and Strong Coloring:**

Robert De Niro, Colin Powell, Ben Affleck, Elvis, Sean Connery, Antonio Banderas, Larry King, Muhammed Ali, Tom Hanks, Tom Cruz, Andrea Bocelli, Benjamin Bratt, Rudi Giuliani, Jackie Chan, Mick Jagger, Lenny Kravitz, John Quinois, John Yang, Will Smith, Kevin Spacey, Rob Lowe, Edward James Olmos, President Ronald Reagan, and John Travolta.

Natural hair colors are dark brown or black. Skin tones range from clear ivory, clear camel, and clear olive to clear dark brown.

◆ **LIGHT-BRIGHT COLOR TYPES—Bright, but Subtle, Clear Colors and Subtle Coloring:**

Tiger Woods, Tom Brokaw, Pete Sampras, Ricky Martin, Tiki and Ronde Barber, George Lopez, Robert Redford, Rod Stewart, President George W. Bush, President Bill Clinton, Barry White, Julio Iglesias, John Tesh, Cuba Gooding, Jr., Greg Norman, B.B. King, Prince William, Denzel Washington, Sting, Danny Glover, and Tom Brady.

Natural hair colors range from golden blond to black (but do not include red). Skin tones range from clear ivory, clear golden ivory, and clear golden camel to clear dark brown with probable golden tones.

◆ **GENTLE COLOR TYPES—Toned Down, Subdued Colors and Subtle Coloring:**

Peter Jennings, Kobe Bryant, Matt Damon, Robin Williams, Michael J. Fox, Sinbad, Rhys Ifans, Jon Bon Jovi, Vladimir Putin, Ron Howard, Nick Carter, Woody Allen, Russell Simmons, Johnny Carson, Stephen Chow, Damon Dash, Kevin Bacon, Mathieu Kassovitz, Sean Combs, Scott Hamilton, and Harrison Ford.

Natural hair colors range from blond to black and include some redheads. Skin tones range from ivory and pink beige to dark brown with probable pink tones.

◆ **MUTED COLOR TYPES—Slightly Toned Down Colors and Strong Coloring:**

Michael Jordan, President John F. Kennedy, Elton John, Jesse Martin, Benicio Del Toro, Steven Weber, Prince Harry, Justin Timberlake, Ted Koppel, Patrick Swayze, Al Gore, Michael Douglas, Nick Lachey, James Blake, Gary Dourdan, Bill Cosby, Russell Crowe, and Damian Lewis.

Natural hair colors range from blond to black and include some redheads. Skin tones range from ivory beige to golden beige and from olive to dark brown.

When your hair turns gray, silver, white, or turns up missing, your Color Type stays the same. Sun-damaged skin, skin rashes/diseases, high doses of some chemicals, and some vitamins *might* change the color of your skin tone and, if permanent, *might* change your Color Type. — JoAnna

Cross Color Types

There are as many Cross Color Types as there are straight Color Types (I'm not talking about lifestyle preferences). Here are some *smart tips* to help you find yourself:

◆ **Contrast/Muted Color Types** might look just like a straight Contrast Color Type, but instead of clear colors, they look best in slightly toned down colors. The natural hair color is very dark brown (with probable reddish highlights) or black.

◆ **Muted/Contrast Color Types**, on the other hand, look best in clear colors instead of slightly toned down colors. They are not straight Contrast Color Types because their color combinations, although gutsy, need to look more "muted." The natural hair color is dark brown (with possible reddish highlights) or black.

◆ **Contrast/Light-Bright Color Types** have half-strong, half-subtle looking coloring and may need to *slightly* take the edge off their clear bold colors, making them just a hint more subtle looking. The natural hair color is very dark brown (with probable golden highlights) or black.

◆ **Light-Bright/Contrast Color Types** have half-subtle, half-strong looking coloring and usually need slightly more powerful color combinations than a straight Light-Bright Color Type. The natural hair color is brown to dark brown (with golden highlights) or black.

◆ **Light-Bright/Gentle Color Types** might look like a straight Light-Bright Color Type, but they need slightly toned down colors instead of clear and bright, yet subtle looking colors. Natural hair colors range from blond to black but do not include redheads.

◆ **Gentle/Light-Bright Color Types** need clear, yet subtle looking bright colors instead of a straight Gentle Color Type's toned down colors. Natural hair colors range from blond to black but do not include redheads.

◆ **Gentle/Muted Color Types** have half-subtle, half-strong coloring, so some of the very blended small patterns that look wonderful on a straight Gentle Color Type may look weak—strengthen color combinations when necessary. Natural hair colors range from blond to black and include some redheads.

◆ **Muted/Gentle Color Types** have half-strong and half-subtle coloring, so some of the darker or gutsier color combinations that look so rich on straight Muted Color Types may look heavy or overpowering.

Lighten darker, or stronger looking, color combinations when necessary. Natural hair colors range from blond to black and include some
redheads.

LOOKING POWERFUL OR WEAK

JUST THE BASICS

◆   Avoid wearing navy and white or black and white together unless
     you know the combination is not overpowering your coloring.

BEYOND THE BASICS

Yet another *technical* thing to discuss—the powerful look of "high-contrast."
Believe me, I wouldn't be writing about it if it weren't very important. How
important? If 50% of you do "it," you will be looking weak instead of powerful.

The highest contrast is created by wearing black or navy with white,
soft white, off-white, and winter-white. Some of you just realized that I am
saying that you may not look great in a navy suit with a white shirt. In a
minute I will explain how you *can* wear this classic business color combination and look **good** (note I did not say great).

All three Contrast Color Types and all three Light-Bright Color Types
look exceptional in high-contrast. However, all three Gentle and all three
Muted Color Types, are overpowered by these high-contrast color combinations—that means that if you are wearing them (just them) and you walk
into a room, your outfit will visually enter ahead of you. They tend to give you
a headless person look.

How can Muted and Gentle Color Types keep this from happening?

1.   Avoid all pure white shirts.

2.   Wear a cream, beige/ecru shirt with a navy or black suit.

3.   If you want to wear a soft white shirt (instead of cream, beige/
     ecru) with a black or navy suit, the colors in your tie become
     very important—find one that has just a touch of the softer white
     of the shirt color in it as well as some of the navy or black of
     your suit and any "other colors" that look great on you. Wearing
     a tie with other colors in it helps "soften" the color combination
     which is no longer JUST navy (or black) and soft white. The
     look will still be powerful on you, just not overpowering.

Not sure about your Color Type? Your mirror will tell you if you need to
soften or avoid high-contrast—try it and see where your eye goes. Put on
a white shirt and a navy jacket and see if your eye goes to the color com-

bination before it goes to you. If it does, you are one of the Gentle or Muted Color Types. Substitute cream or your best light beige/ecru shirt for the white and look at the **spectacular difference**. For you, slightly softer contrast makes for a much more powerful, authoritative entrance than walking in without your head.

SUBTLE AND STRONG

JUST THE BASICS

◆   If your coloring is *subtle* looking (Light-Bright and Gentle Color Types), you will want to make all of your color combinations subtle looking also—Light-Bright Color Types need "crispness," as well. If your coloring is *strong* (all Muted and Contrast Color Types), your color combinations will need more strength.

BEYOND THE BASICS

Picture it. If you have a painting that needs to be framed, you would never pick out a powerful, bold-looking frame for a subtle-looking watercolor. Nor would you select a subtle looking, delicate frame for a bold graphic.

If your *coloring* is subtle (this term has nothing to do with your personality), **lighten up darker colors and dark, or strong, color combinations.** You could also avoid wearing them.

If your *coloring* is stronger, gutsier looking, it's not necessary for you to lighten strong color combinations, but you will probably need to **strengthen** or **brighten** other *specific* color combinations.

If you are a Contrast Color Type, you will need to add a light or bright accent to an all-dark color combination—the exception is black **if** you look good in it head-to-toe. Also, add a bright or dark accent to an all-light color combination or just avoid wearing them—the exception is all white or all cream.

If you are a Muted Color Type you will not need to lighten dark color combinations **unless your hair is light**. If your hair is medium to dark in tone, you may need to strengthen light color combinations (add a medium or dark color) or wear them in large blocks of color. Avoid wearing small patterns that combine light colors—they aren't gutsy enough for you.

By the way, you do know by now that having strong or subtle coloring has nothing to do with your personality or body shape and size, right?

Changing the Way
the World Looks at You

Classic and *Classy*

> There is an art to being timeless, yet so current that you look like your *knowledge and skills* are up to the minute. — JoAnna

Just the Basics

- If you want your suits, jackets, trousers, shirts, and ties to look suitable for several years, avoid buying fads, extremes in fashion, or anything flashy.

Beyond the Basics

> Being *contemporary* is always in style, but to be considered fashionable one does not need to wear the current looks shown on the runway or in fashion magazines, spend a lot of money, be thin, or young. — JoAnna

Classic styles have perennial appeal, a long life expectancy, and they are used every day in some way by most of us. Classics look stylish for decades, depending on the ways in which you combine them with each other or with newer "fashions."

Instead of telling you what is classic, it's easier to describe what **isn't**:

- Oversized, extremely wide lapels.
- Undersized, very narrow lapels.
- Oversized, wide ties.
- Very narrow ties.
- Shirts with long pointed collars.

- 👁 Extreme spread or very widespread collars.

- 👁 Very narrow trousers.

- 👁 Very wide trousers.

- 👁 Sleeves with ruffles that come down to your knuckles (just kidding and wanted to see if you're paying attention).

- 👁 Anything too flashy.

- 👁 Shoes with very square or very pointed toes.

- 👁 Jackets much longer than just covering your seat.

- 👁 Any double-breasted jacket with more, or fewer, than 6 buttons.

- 👁 A double-breasted jacket with a button-down shirt.

- 👁 Any single-breasted jacket with more, or fewer, than 2 or 3 buttons.

- 👁 Anything too complicated.

Sometimes something is considered classic in a certain region of our country but not in another. For example, in parts of the west and southwest, western attire is classic, but not in New York City (except for jeans, which are classic everywhere).

Funky is a wonderfully broad term that seems to be classic for some teens and, depending on the item, is a fad or fashion for the rest of us.

Fashion-forward to the new *silhouettes:* The suits today have more of a personality. Many jackets used to be cut straight up and down and they looked boxy (and could do the same to the wearer)—that's how they got the name "sack suit."

The silhouette that replaced the sack suit is the *soft suit*. Nipped at the waist, these suits no longer look like a sack, and they can be found in 2-button and 3-button styling. The contouring at the waist creates a V shape where the shoulder looks broader than the waistline—it is a super classic look, always has been. It's just been pushed into the forefront of fashion today—so it looks new again.

Fads definitely make a statement but is it a *smart* statement for you to make? Fads usually have a shorter life expectancy and a young following. They are generally considered wild, far-out, or over-the-top by current standards. However, it is possible that they may stand the test of time, become a *fashion* and maybe even a *classic*. After all, there has been some movement and change since the time of your father and grandfather, it's just slow. Unless your job calls for it now, keep fads for your free time.

Please note that *classic* and *boring* are not synonyms. — JoAnna

---

LOOK *SMART*—BUY *SMART* 💰

JUST THE BASICS

- To get the most versatility out of your clothing, buy *smart basics* in solid colors in fabrics that can be combined and worn all, or almost all, year.

BEYOND THE BASICS

If you're on a budget and want every purchase to count, buy *smart basics*. Besides being classic in styling, what makes a garment a *smart basic*? All of the following:

- It's as solid a color as possible, meaning that it was made out of matching fibers/yarns/threads versus those that have even the slightest variation in tone.

- All stitching matches the garment exactly.

- The color of the buttons match the garment exactly.

- There are no extra details on the garment like epaulets or a contrasting color.

- Its fabric can be combined with many other fabrics.

- At least three-season weight.

- It is styled in such a way that it can be worn with many different things.

- Nothing is very oversized or undersized, such as collars or lapels.

- It's perfectly plain and simple—do not think boring—think *easy elegance.*

You can create outstanding style with *classic* basics that you can wear for years and years—it's all in how you choose to combine them for your coloring that makes the difference between looking okay and looking fabulous.

LOOKING AS IF YOU DON'T HAVE A CLUE 🔍

JUST THE BASICS

- To look great every day, all you need is to learn a new skill.

- You don't know what you don't know.

BEYOND THE BASICS

You are just beginning to know what you don't. No one can dress well without training or without a full-length mirror. Think about training for a minute and about how you would perform in your job if you hadn't been trained to do it. **Dressing smart** is the same principle. Just because you are smart and very competent doesn't mean that you should be able to dress yourself without learning the skill—the art.

For example, every man can use a keyboard. Yes, you can. Those of you who took lessons type faster and more accurately than those of you who haven't had lessons—without lessons, you can still type, but this is called the hunt and peck method. With your wardrobe, I call it "hit and miss."

If you've had typing lessons, do you remember your first test? I think that I clocked in at 17 words a minute and made five mistakes. By my second test, I was up to 35 words a minute with three mistakes. *Eventually,* with practice, 80 words a minute, nearly perfect. After lessons, if using a keyboard is part of your life, you just get better and better at it.

A full-length mirror helps you train your eye and gives you a true reflection of your appearance, but you need to be willing to take a **good** look. It's always how you feel in something that counts the most, but sometimes it takes looking at yourself in a photo or on a TV screen to realize you need to make a change. A distinguished man called to book an appointment with me after he saw himself on the evening news and didn't like what he saw!

> After his initial lesson with me, he bought some suits and ties recommended by a salesperson at a prestigious men's store and brought them to me to check them. He had been sold suits that were toned down, very blended looking (perfect for Peter Jennings's coloring), when *he* needed solid colors so he could create high-contrast looks. We reviewed his best color combinations and he instantly understood the difference—those suits were returned and replaced with suits that were perfect for *him*.

To train your eye, you must look carefully at yourself often. Women are a bit better at this because they are used to trying on clothes, looking in the mirror, taking them off and trying something else on—they are *willing* to do this, and you may want to consider doing this, willingly or not. I know that you check yourself out in the gym (because I'm there three days a week watching you), and this isn't much different. You just need to know what to check out—and it's not from just the neck down. Any man can put on a suit and tie and match his belt to his shoes. That doesn't mean he looks good!

One man can look at himself in a mirror and say, "I look fine," when he really doesn't. Perhaps his tie doesn't look good with his suit but he doesn't perceive this. This man knows **less** than the man who looks in the mirror and says, "Something isn't working but I don't know what."

Your level of knowledge is higher when you can tell what's **wrong**— "The colors in my tie are fine with this suit and the suit is fine with my shirt, but together it just doesn't look coordinated." You are even *smarter* yet when you know how to fix the problem—"I need to change my tie to one that has some of my suit color and some of the color of my shirt in it."

A MIRROR IMAGE

JUST THE BASICS

♨ Studying your image in a full-length mirror will help you know at a glance if you look great, just okay, or not so good.

BEYOND THE BASICS

Why do you have to train your eye? Because you can't trust everything you are told, what you see on a store mannequin, or everything you read. The old adage is true—just because you see it in print doesn't make it so. To start training your eye, you want to learn to do a "mirror test." Walk a few paces away from a floor-length mirror—good lighting helps. Turn around *fast.* If your eye goes immediately to your white shirt (like it's popping out), you need soft white shirts instead. More on that later. If your eye goes instantly to the color or pattern in your tie, it is probably too bright, too bold, and/or too large a pattern for you, causing you to look overdone or garish—certainly not a successful look.

If your glance reveals an overall washed-out or dull look, the color or pattern of your tie is more than likely too muted, too weak, and/or too quiet looking for you. Looking drab or mousy is not a healthy, successful look!

Learn to use your mirror to your advantage and let it help educate you. Check everything:

- [ ] Are your thick-soled wing tip shoes too heavy looking for your tropical-weight suit?

- [ ] Is your tie tied too short, too long?

- [ ] Are your colors balanced and coordinated looking?

- [ ] Do they really enhance you?

- [ ] Does your face look washed-out?

- [ ] Does your hair style make the statement **you** want?

- [ ] Do **you** love the way you look?

- [ ] Would you be happy about the way you are dressed if you suddenly happen to meet the president of the company you've always wanted to work for, or you are stuck in the elevator with *that* woman from the 6th floor?

LETTING GO OF LIMITATIONS,

 BAD ADVICE, & OLD MYTHS

JUST THE BASICS

 You can create any look and wear any style you wish, as long as you get the scale, fit, and balance right for your size and shape.

BEYOND THE BASICS

Yes, you can. All you need are a few lessons (*smart tips*), your sense of humor, a full-length mirror, patience, perseverence, the willingness to train your eye, and a good tailor.

If your size and/or shape have been a limitation to you in the past, it has only been because your head has been filled with less than accurate advice and a mind-set of old myths. You need confidence and knowledge to challenge myths and years of bad advice. If you are full-bodied or below average in height, your life has probably been filled with so many *DON'TS* that you've had very few *DO'S* to work with—a vast injustice, because you can *DO* everything every other man can—it's all a matter of proportion for you, specifically.

 Bad Advice: Tall men should accentuate width by having a sloped shoulder look; loose waist; pocket flaps; wearing patterns, checks, and tweeds; not wearing a 3-button jacket; and they should wear spread collars.

 More Bad Advice: If you are heavy, wear long pointed collars and bold ties and do not wear double-breasted jackets, narrow-toed shoes or small size jewelry because it will look too dainty.

 Even More Bad Advice: If you are below average in height, wear only square shoulders and long pointed collars.

 And Yet More Bad Advice: If you are well built (muscular), wear single-breasted jackets in dark colors to minimize bulk and hide your build and wear jackets with a low button stance.

 My Advice: It wouldn't be nice to tell you what I'm really thinking so I'll just say—WHAT WERE THE AUTHORS OF THIS HORRIFIC ADVICE THINKING?

Dress to look great every day, not to look taller or slimmer. All men of every height and hunk (oh, so sorry) width can look wonderful in all styles including a double-breasted jacket—it's all in the fit and proportion of the garment. Double-breasted for fuller figured men, also? Yes, definitely. It's a super look **IF** it fits you perfectly. Very elegant men come in all sizes and shapes. Regardless of your size and the jacket style you are wearing, if the buttons pull or the lapels gape open, you will look larger and like you have outgrown your clothes—less elegant than you would wish.

TAILORED TO DISTINCTION

JUST THE BASICS

✂ Jacket length long enough to just cover your seat.

✂ Jacket fits in shoulders—or do not buy.

✂ Jacket collar lies perfectly against shirt collar at back of neck.

✂ Jacket is slightly defined at the waist.

✂ Sleeve ends slightly below wrist bone.

✂ Trouser cuff covers the back of shoe.

✂ Waistband is at navel with the rise neither too long nor too short.

BEYOND THE BASICS

When it comes to style, any silhouette can look good on you. How is this possible? It's the fit, the silhouette that works for **your** proportion that creates elegance. You are training your eye to work with your own body and your unique coloring.

There is an important visual difference between tailored clothing that looks like it was made for you and something that is *almost* right. Not many men can put a jacket on and walk out of the store looking fabulous.

Take the time and money to get it more than right—you will never regret it. Expensive garments will look less expensive if they fit poorly, and less expensive garments can look *more* expensive (if the fabric is good) when they are tailored to fit you.

When you went to purchase your first suit or jacket, you got measured by the salesperson, who then told you what size you wear. There is a chance that you are a different size now—maybe you've filled out a little. Regardless of the size you try on, only **you** know how a garment feels on the *inside* and how you feel about yourself when you look in the mirror. It could look good but feel tight, and it could feel wonderful but look too small or too big—or just not be the image you want for yourself right now.

It's best not to consider any jacket that doesn't fit well in the shoulders, isn't a good length, or stands away from the back of your neck. Each can be changed, but it's not easy and therefore is expensive. Jackets/blazers should fit with enough ease that they can be worn over a sweater—not a bulky sweater—but those that are lighter weight, such as a fine merino wool or up to a 3-ply cashmere.

Develop a good relationship with a skilled tailor. One of the perks from purchasing suits, jackets, and trousers from a department store, like Macy's or Nordstrom, or a men's specialty store, for example, is that most alterations will be done very professionally for no extra charge. At Nordstrom, not only do they cuff trousers and make sure your sleeve length is perfect, they will take jackets and trousers in or let them out, move buttons, add brace buttons, and close a vent if you want them to. If you don't like the buttons, they will charge you about $10 to change them. A lot of confidence is derived from knowing that your clothing has been tailored to fit you perfectly.

Things to tailor when necessary include:

✂ Shape and general fit of jacket including any collar roll (excess fabric in the back of the suit just below the collar). The fabric needs to lie smoothly and the collar itself should lie against your shirt collar, not stand away from it. Sometimes there is an extra charge for this.

✂ Sleeve length.

✂ Trouser length.

✂ Waist taken in or out so pockets don't spread.

✂ Seat taken in or out—including altering the rise.

✂ Trousers narrowed—tapered to perfect scale for your leg length.

✂ Buttons moved or changed.

Your jacket sleeve should cover your wrist bone and fall into the indentation where your thumb and your wrist bone join. Sleeves that are too short can give you an awkward, gangly look—not elegant. Sleeves that are too long can throw off your body proportions, causing you to look squat (ah, I finally found another word for dumpy), as can trousers that are too wide in the upper leg and/or at the cuff.

Always have the hem/cuff marked with your shoes on. You will have to put yourself in control of the length—even though you may say you like a slight break, medium break, or full break, you need to check it. Not much is worse (less elegant looking) than wearing your trousers too short so your socks show (even when you are walking) unless you are Fred Astaire or Gene Kelly and you want people to watch your feet.

It's personal preference, but I recommend at least a medium break just to get your trousers long enough in the back—none of my experts favor no break and I adamantly agree. The bottom **in the back** should just cover, or come to, the seam/crack/groove where the heel of the shoe meets the sole. Aim for about 1" off the floor in the back. Stand on a flat solid surface when your pants are marked, not on a carpet. Without a cuff, the hem of your trousers can be angled up to 3/4" to make them longer in the back, if you wish.

Arm holes can be deepened if they are too small/tight to give you more room. Shoulders can be altered, but it's a big (expensive) job so it's best if the shoulders fit perfectly to begin with.

How does the jacket hang when it's unbuttoned? A jacket that is too big in the hips (sometimes referred to as having too much fabric in the skirt of the jacket) can create a stodgy look. I wish that I could come up with different words than "stodgy," "frumpy," and "dowdy," but I haven't. You have to admit that they are pretty descriptive.

Don't forget to check the mirror for the way you look from the side and back. Clothes that fit too tight can make you look like you just gained several pounds even if you've just lost 10—they actually make you look bigger instead of smaller. Sometimes a jacket looks as if it fits perfectly from a front view but from a side view you'll see too much fullness in the back. It's easy to remedy—*please* have it done, as it will make all the difference in the world between your looking ordinary and looking extraordinary—a much better description than stodgy.

Do fill your jacket and pant pockets with your toys (wallet/handheld computer/phone) before having the tailor begin—he needs to allow room for them.

Bulging pockets, even if they are filled with money, give an inelegant look even to an expensive suit. If you are trying to carry as much as a woman carries in her handbag, you may be looking "lumpy," as bad a word as frumpy.

You're a problem solver, so I have confidence that you can solve this problem. Sort it all out, carry only what you need, and think about how you can better disperse the rest. Maybe a longer, slimmer wallet for a breast pocket is the answer for those of you who carry a lot of cards, but then where would you put your cell and palm? Would a money clip help? I once went to a formal affair (there were princes and princesses in the room) with a guy whose chest looked bigger than mine—on one side. When I asked him what was in the breast pocket of his tuxedo he showed me his wallet. It was stuffed with everything but the kitchen sink—and its crowning glory was a rubber band that held it all together!

FABRICATING STYLE

JUST THE BASICS

- ♠ Wear 100% wool, other natural fibers, or blends of natural with a small percentage of manmade fibers.

- ♠ Nice hand (feels good to touch).

    ♣ Drapes well.

    ♣ Good weight for your climate.

BEYOND THE BASICS

There are many, many suit fabrics and you really don't need to know what they are called (like a calvary twill that is softer and finer than it used to be but now so hard to find). What you always want, regardless of what a fabric or weave is called, is a suit or jacket that has a nice hand, drapes well, is styled to suit your body and your career needs, is comfortable, resilient, and durable—equally.

A nice *hand* means it feels good to the touch—just walk down a row of suits or jackets and touch them and you'll understand this word. The experience will also keep you from ever buying one that you wouldn't want to touch. Don't buy a garment if it is scratchy—you'll avoid wearing it. And, no, unfortunately it won't feel any better when it's cold outside.

The *drape* is the way a fabric hangs on your body—generally you can count on fabrics that have a nice hand to drape well versus looking too stiff or too flimsy. *Durability* is, of course, how well the suit will wear—not how long you can wear it until it falls apart. *Resilience* means that the fabric will bounce back, avoiding wrinkles, so you will look as good going into an afternoon meeting as you did when you got dressed in the morning.

If you live in a moderate or hot climate, it's so easy—all of your wool suits, blazers, and odd jackets can be tropical-weight. If you live in a climate that has four distinct seasons, you will need both tropical-weight and heavier weight wools.

For added interest, you can wear different textures together, such as wool flannel trousers with a jacket in one of the more flat fine weaves. When the look doesn't jive it's usually because a light-weight fabric is being mixed with one that is heavy, or a distinctly spring/summer garment is worn with one that is definitely a fall/winter look.

Similar weights of fabrics easily balance each other, like pairing two light-weight fabrics. It's also possible to combine most light-weight fabrics with medium-weight fabrics, and most medium-weight fabrics with heavier weight fabrics without looking out of sync.

For example, a wool flannel jacket could look too heavy with tropical-weight wool trousers, but a wool crepe jacket would look fine; a linen shirt is too light-weight and summery looking to wear with a heavier weight wool and cashmere blazer. When balance is thrown off in this way, sometimes the less substantial fabric can end up looking inexpensive—even if it isn't. This look has a better chance of working if the heavier fabric is on the bottom and the lighter on the top.

Mix fabrics and textures (and styles) that make the same *statement*. Dressy sea island shirts and high-sheen silk ties are good together but don't mix well with casual looking suit and jacket fabrics. Neither do French cuffs.

The most desirable suit fabrics today are called the **super 100's**—it has to do with the grade of the wool. Even though most of the suits you will want are 100% wool, you will also find super suits and jackets in cashmere, of course, and in blends of wool with cashmere, silk, rayon, nylon, and so on—even some with a very small percentage of lycra/spandex. Ah, spandex—get your mind back on your wardrobe, and there may be more spandex in your future.

   Ⓝ **Bad Advice?** Corduroy is business-like.

   ① **My Advice:** It is business casual, never dressier. Some books advise (but not my experts) that it is a year-round fabric—it is for fall/winter, or cool weather, only.

If your *coloring* is subtle looking, it's best for you to avoid really rough, coarse fabrics and very heavy-looking textures.

Any fabric that "looks" casual is best avoided for strictly business looks. The following are generally considered casual fabrics but with new technology, some may be found to be quite dressy looking: cottons in general, khaki, chino, rayon, denim, and corduroy (which comes in three different wales, the narrowest of which is the most flattering to all Color Types while those of you with Light-Bright and Gentle coloring should avoid the wide wales). The advances in what can be done with cotton is amazing—it can even be woven to look like wool and yet feel like heaven.

The seersucker suit is a summer classic, but among my experts there are differing opinions on the best way to wear it. One says it's better kept together as a suit than just wearing the jacket as an odd jacket. Another says it is best, now, to just wear the jacket with different trousers or with jeans. I say, therefore, that you can wear it as you like it best. For example, the classic blue and white seersucker jacket with a white or soft white shirt (depending on the look you want, collar band, classic pointed collar, or *nice* T-shirt) and blue jeans; blue trousers the same color as the blue stripe (or a touch darker); or with white or soft white trousers. Follow the same idea for other seersucker color combinations.

Cotton suits (can you believe it?) are coming into their own for hot weather, and some of them are superb looking. Still think they would look *cheap*? Armani made one for $2,225.00—I added the zeros so you would know the price isn't a typo. Just as with any fabric for any item of clothing, judge by the way it looks on you, the way it feels, and by how you feel in it. One of my guy friends, shopping with me, bought an awesome cotton designer jacket for $55. I didn't even have to twist his arm. The majority of cotton suits, no matter what they cost, are not as dressy as wool. No dressy-looking ties or French cuffs with them, please.

Can you wear **linen** to work? Yes, as long as you are willing to accept the following truism: Linen wrinkles. Wrinkled linen is charming. If you need perfection, don't wear it. If you feel that it wouldn't be appropriate for a serious meeting, don't wear it for those occasions.

Microfiber has become a generic term for manmade fabrics, which are getting better and better, but they still don't *breathe* (let the air through) so they can be hot or make you feel sticky. Some forward-looking styles are being made in these fabrics, so if you want to try them out—in pants for example—make sure they have a good hand. Even though they are getting better, some can look, or feel, too stiff, so they don't drape well on the body—others just feel "cheesy." Also, some microfibers have a bit too much shine under certain lights.

Occasionally you will see even 100% wool suits in **shiny fabrics**. They are too flashy for most men, especially in the daytime. Unless you are in a profession that would find this look a plus, wear it strictly in the evening and keep your shirt and all of your accessories equally as dressy but understated. There is a difference between a "sheen" (a good word) and "shiny" (a bad word—in this case).

Any suit that has been wrinkled on purpose before you buy it is best kept for those of you who need this look to successfully further your funky-dresser image.

Interpreting Patterns

"I want something other than a solid or a stripe." Or, "I want something different." That's how many men let the salesperson know that they are interested in looking at a *pattern* like a check, tweed, herringbone, or plaid suit or jacket.

Here's another *very* important detail. All patterns should have at least two of your best colors prominent in them, AND the background color should also be flattering to you. A reminder that Light-Bright and Gentle Color Types are easily over-powered by too much "going on," too busy a pattern, too much overall pattern, or too many colors—too overdone.

> No button-down shirt with a pin-striped or chalk-striped/hairline-striped suit—the shirt is too casual for the suit. — JoAnna

The stripe in the pinstripe is made from a series of little dots. When the dots are white, on a black or navy background, they give this suit a very high-contrast look that is only worn well by Contrast and Light-Bright Color Types. Light-Bright Color Types need the stripes to be less apparant and more closely spaced or the suit can look too bold or busy on them.

The chalk-stripe (just picture a chalk line), sometimes harder to find than the pinstripe, can be elegant without being as showy because the line is softer, more diffused looking. There is one concern. This stripe is often more widely spaced, creating a larger pattern look that many men are uncomfortable wearing. From a Color Type perspective, only Contrast Color Types can handle the wider stripes, especially those that are high-contrast. All wide-spaced stripes can be a concern for Light-Bright, Gentle, or Muted coloring if the overall look is that of a large pattern.

The hairline-stripe is so narrow that it is less in your face and, depending on the color combination, will work for all Color Types.

A white stripe on any color other than navy or black—gray, for example—is fine for all Color Types. When the stripe is any color other than white, the suit has the possibility of working for all Color Types, depending on the colors and shirt and tie combination you wear with it. With any stripe a good guideline is: the wider the stripe, the more subtle (faint) the stripe should appear. When the stripe and the background colors blend together, the look is more subtle and wearable for all.

> An elegant guideline: The wider the stripe, the more subtle it should be. *Discretion is preferred for all elegance.* —Joseph Farnel

Now that we've discussed them, I'd like to say that even on the right Color Type, I'm not the hugest fan of sharp black and white or dark navy and white stripes that you can see coming from a block away. I know that they are classic and traditional and I know that some of you have a desire for variety. But there is a very fine line between looking sharp and looking like a sharpie that I think the sharp stripes cross. If you understand what I just said, you understand understated elegance—to look sharp, your suit will never scream or walk into a room ahead of you.

All Contrast and Light-Bright Color Types should avoid purchasing any blended looking patterns/weaves (because they will look drab on them) which include many, but not all, glen plaids, pheasant's eye/birds eye, nailhead, tweed, herringbone, and houndstooth. The exceptions here are those done in more crisp contrast like black, or navy, with what might appear as "white." Regardless of your Color Type, don't expect a pure white (or sometimes even a soft white) shirt to work with any blended looking fabric, even those that have white in them. Why? Because white wool fibers are not pure white and even if they are *fairly white*, once they get woven with another color, the overall look is more attractive with softer whites and cream.

Any time you see different colors in a suit (even just two different colors) it will be more difficult to find the perfect tie. Some salespeople, and books, will suggest you wear these blended looks with brightly colored ties and bright striped shirts—PLEASE DON'T. Even though this look was "traditional," it doesn't mean that it ever looked good from either a style or color standpoint. Paraphrasing what Thomas Jefferson said, just because something has been done a certain way for a long time, doesn't make it right for today, and it doesn't mean that it was ever right.

In case you need to know, nailhead is a design of woven dots about the size of a nailhead; birds eye/pheasant's eye is a diamond shape weave; herringbone is a diagonal texture that looks like "V"; and houndstooth is a weave of tiny checks. Tweeds are woven without a pattern and will have two or more different colored yarns.

Touted by some experts (not me) as the second suit to buy after navy is a nailhead. Unless they are in a black and white, navy and white or a dark gray and white weave, these blended looking fabrics are difficult for Contrast and Light-Bright Color Types to work with. Those that are black and white or navy and white are generally not enhancing to Gentle or Muted Color Types. Keep in mind that it is often more difficult to find perfect ties for any blended look.

Have a blended looking suit like this that you need a tie for? If you are a Gentle or Muted Color Type, you'll look for a blended looking tie with some of your best colors in it as well as a touch of the suit color—your shirt could be one of the colors in the tie or suit, or perhaps a soft white, depending on which gives the overall best effect. If you are a Contrast or Light-Bright Color Type, find a tie that has some visual contrast with some of your best clear colors in it as well as a touch of the suit color—your shirt could be one of the colors in the tie, the suit, or maybe soft white, depending on which gives the overall best effect.

Make a dummy of yourself on the bed (sorry, *create* a mockup) and check it out. This suit fabric is generally not good with a pure white shirt as the shirt makes the suit look dirty or drab by comparison.

The third suit some experts (again, not me) want you to buy is a pin-stripe, which you just read about, or a muted windowpane. Windowpanes most often have a solid background woven with lines of a different color that form boxes that resemble, you guessed it, windowpanes. The boxes can be very small or very large and the color combinations range from high-contrast to blended subtle looks. When buying this pattern, keep in mind your Color Type and your best color combinations.

The fourth suit some experts want you to buy is a mini check or a glen plaid. Glen plaids come in different color combinations—the plaid is formed by several small vertical and horizontal lines. Finding a compatible tie is difficult, let alone finding one that looks good on **you** and the colors in the suit pattern. Please follow my guidelines for the nailhead fabric above.

If a pattern size is too small for you, it can make you look totally insignificant—the opposite of a **powerful**, successful image. If a pattern size is too large for you, it can completely OVERPOWER you, making you look washed-out by comparison. Don't be afraid of stripes, plaids, and patterns—just learn which ones will flatter you. No, you don't ever have to wear them if you don't want to.

Patterned After Perfection

Just the Basics

⚓ The right pattern size will help you look exceptional—the wrong size will keep you from being noticed.

BEYOND THE BASICS

I'll bet you think that pattern size has to do with your height and body structure. Enhancing pattern size has to do with your body *coloring*. Yes, I know this is contrary to what you may believe, but it's true. Except for "placement," pattern size has nothing to do with how tall you are or aren't, **or** with your size or shape.

Everyone can wear medium-sized patterns, but not everyone looks good in *small*, quiet patterns or LARGE patterns. There are always a couple of "it depends upon."

If your coloring is more subtle-looking, Gentle and Light-Bright Color Types, you'll look terrific in small and medium-sized patterns, and (here's one of the it depends upon) very light-weight, subtle-looking, larger patterns that have a light background. Light-Bright Color Types will want to avoid small patterns that are *blended* looking (where all of the colors seem to run together) and, instead, choose those that have explicit, crisp contrast.

Those of you who are Muted Color Types look good in medium-sized patterns, small patterns that have some strength, GUTSINESS, and (another it depends upon) very *blended* looking larger patterns.

If you are a Contrast Color Type, medium and large patterns look super on you. Small patterns that have explicit, crisp contrast or combine dark colors with bright colors will also look good—no toned down colors or quiet patterns, please.

If you are a full-bodied Contrast Color Type who is concerned about wearing large patterns, just be aware of **where** you place them on your body. In a tie, it's always fine. The idea is to look great at any size—not to try to hide a husky body behind a weak patterned tie that looks wimpy and ineffective on you. If you are below average in height and a Contrast Color Type, and are worried that large patterns will overwhelm you, don't be. The proof will be in the compliments you get when you finally decide to wear a *color-perfect* pattern.

What About Your Personality?

If you happen to have a big pattern tie personality but have coloring that looks best with small and medium-sized patterns, the tie will look like it has taken on a personality of its own—a goofy one. The same tie that would look elegant on a man with Contrast coloring can have this effect on Light-Bright, Gentle and Muted Color Types. Gentle and Light-Bright Color Types best chance of looking good in a larger patterned tie would be to select one that has a light background and a very light-weight, airy looking pattern. For Muted Color Types, larger pattern ties should have a *blended* look. If on the other hand you have a small subtle patterned tie personality but coloring that needs a gutsier look lest you appear washed-out or ineffective, keep your small patterns as strong as possible with colors that have contrast versus colors that all blend together.

Contrast and Light-Bright Color Types should avoid ties that are toned down or muted looking because they will look insignificant and drab on you while ties with clear colors will give you a healthy, successful look. Gentle and Muted Color Types should avoid ties with clear, bright colors because they will overpower you. The ties that will look terrific on you will have toned down, muted colors. Gentle and Muted Color Types also need to avoid ties that are black and white or navy and white unless the tie has additional colors that are toned down to help soften the contrast.

Peter Jennings, Kobe Bryant, and Vladimir Putin wouldn't look good in ties that look super on Larry King, Benjamin Bratt, Jon Yang, or Will Smith. Michael Jordan, Benicio Del Toro, and Michael Douglas shouldn't share ties with George Bush, Tiger Woods, George Lopez, or Ricky Martin. Remember, there are no single categories for **all** blonds, brunettes, black hair, or redheads, nor are there for **all** Black, Asian, Hispanic, Native American, or Caucasian men.

To help you make the best possible impact, here are your best *color combinations* by Color Type:

 Contrast Color Types

◆ Wear a dark color with a bright color.

◆ Wear a bright color with a light color.

◆ Wear two bright colors together.

◆ Wear a dark color with a light color.

◆ Avoid using two light colors together without adding a bright or dark color.

◆ Avoid using two dark colors together without adding a light or bright accent.

Light-Bright Color Types

◆ Wear a light color with a bright color.

◆ Wear two medium-toned subtle looking bright colors together.

◆ Wear a dark color with a light color.

◆ If you wear two light colors together, you will probably need to add a contrasting accent (a bright or dark color) near your face.

◆ Avoid wearing a bright color with a dark color without adding a light accent.

◆ Avoid wearing two dark colors together. If you do, you will definitely need to lighten the color combination.

Gentle Color Types

◆ Wear two light colors together.

◆ Wear a light color with a medium color.

◆ Wear two medium colors together.

◆ Wear a medium color with a dark color (light-haired Gentle Color Types will need a light accent near your face).

◆ Wear any dark color with any light color except in the case of high-contrast (see next combination).

◆ Avoid wearing the high-contrast combinations of black, navy, and possibly dark brown, with white/off-white without softening the contrast with a tie—you can use your cream or light beige/ecru or any other light color effectively with navy, black, and dark brown.

◆ Avoid wearing two dark colors together, especially if your hair is light to medium in tone. If you do, you will definitely need to lighten the color combination.

Muted Color Types

◆ Wear a light color with a medium color.

◆ Wear two medium colors together.

◆ Wear a dark color with a medium color.

◆ Wear two light colors together in larger blocks of color or accent lighter color combinations with a medium or dark color.

◆ Wear two dark colors together (light-haired Muted Color Types will need a light or medium accent).

◆ Wear any dark color with any light color except the following.

◆ Avoid wearing the high-contrast color combination of black, navy, and possibly dark brown with white/off-white without softening the contrast with a tie—you can use your cream or light beige/ecru or any other light color effectively with navy, black, and dark brown.

⊘ **Bad Advice:** The more bold the shirt, the more sober the tie.

① **My Advice:** If sober, to you, means a quiet pattern, you'll throw the balance off (i.e., the shirt will look garish and the tie will look washed-out, dirty, old, or drab by comparison). If sober means solid color or classic (i.e., dot or smaller simple pattern with the same colors as shirt and suit), okay.

⊘ **Ridiculous Advice:** In a men's magazine tall men are advised to wear brightly colored shirts and ties and only spread collar shirts.

① **My Advice:** Train your eye so you'll know BS (stands for bad stuff) when you see it or hear it.

⊘ **Bad Advice:** The more sober the shirt, the more bold the tie.

① **My Advice:** In this instance, the tie would look garish and the shirt will look washed-out and drab by comparison. A reminder that no individual looks wonderful in **both** clear, bright colors and muted, toned down colors. A bright red tie doesn't work well on a pale blue shirt because the shirt looks faded by comparison, and that can make the tie look overly bright. Contrast and Light-Bright Color Types, switch to a brighter blue shirt and note the difference—Gentle and Muted Color Types, switch to a less bright tie.

Burgundy, one of the most over-rated colors of the last century, was dubbed a safe, conservative, "neutral," but it just doesn't go with men. Okay, if it's a true burgundy that is the color of a fine wine in a clear glass, Muted and dark-haired Gentle Color Types can *make* it work. Brownish burgundy is not a flattering color for **anyone**—man or woman.

Regardless of what you may have heard or read, the pattern of a shirt and tie can both be in the same scale, small, for example, like a small-check shirt with a small-dot tie. They can also both be checks. And, even though it may be over the top for you and can be difficult to get it perfect, you can pair a striped suit with a striped shirt and a striped tie. It's the color combination that makes the difference and with compatible colors, mixing same, or different, scale and patterns can be done well.

When in doubt, keep it simple and remember that *easy elegance* is never boring. Just because some other men may be more adventuresome (often overly) in their color combinations doesn't mean you must be as well. Both looks, when done with knowledge, judgment, and dash (but not flash), can be exceptional.

Much more important than knowing the difference between a club or regimental tie and a paisley, medallion, or foulard is for you to know which clarity of color and color combinations are best for you and how to combine them with your suits, jackets, trousers, and shirts.

> ⊘ **Bad Advice:** Wear a toned down, blended looking green, black, and blue wool plaid suit with a wool tie (the fact that the tie is wool is super—but wait) that is green, red, orange, yellow, and gray.

> ① **My Advice:** No way! No matter what you have heard, seen, or read, bold ties do not look good with toned down, blended look-ing herringbones and muted plaids. Quieter looking suit fabrics need ties with quiet colors, otherwise your tie will walk into a room ahead of you—it will also look garish.

Solid-color suiting fabrics can be worn with both bright ties or quieter ties—your Color Type determines which will look best on you.

Some of you are still curious about tie patterns. Even though you don't need to know what they are called, familiarity can bring confidence:

◆ Paisley—paramecia-shaped patterns.

◆ Foulard—printed figures on solid background.

◆ Medallion—small medallions placed here and there on a solid background.

◆ Regimental—different colors in differing widths of stripes (each British regiment had their own).

◆ Club—solid background with small design or insignia that re-peats in rows.

◆ Polka-dot—dots on a solid background.

◆ Overall pattern—varying patterns in different sizes and colors.

◆ Solid color with interesting texture.

There are a lot of popular suiting fabrics that men tend to think of as being a solid color but the weave *blends* different fibers together so the color ends up being *not quite* solid. These almost solids are more easily paired with ties that have toned down colors, so they are difficult to work with if you are a Contrast or Light-Bright Color Type. If you are one of these Color Types, look for ties that have clear colors with just a touch of the blended color, or stay in an all-neutral color scheme that has some light-dark contrast including a touch of the color of the suit.

Avoid wearing a tie that has high-contrast—like black and white—with the softer contrast look of a gray stripe suit. If the black and white tie also has a touch of gray, it will work with the suit. If not, find a tie that includes the gray of the suit, the color of the stripe in the suit, and the color of your shirt, and you'll have a superb look.

With suits and jackets in other than solid colors, like tweeds, herringbones, plaids, and checks, some men have been taught to isolate and identify little bits of colors in the fabric with the purpose of trying to find what colors of shirts and ties will work with it. The concern with this method is that often the color(s) is so faint that when you use just that color in a shirt or tie there's no visible relationship. Unless you are just a few inches away, there isn't enough of that color in the suit or jacket that you can even see it. Make sure you look good close up and from a few paces away from your mirror.

Collect perfect ties—look for those that combine touches of all of your suit colors, favorite shirt colors, and trouser colors. For business casual, if you wear khakis and/or jeans, you will want some ties that look more casual. Low-sheen ties have a better chance of working with more casual suits and jackets. Your more casual ties will need to have a touch of the khaki or the colors of your jeans (light, medium, or dark blue, black, gray, and so on) in them as well as your shirt and any jacket color. Bringing even a touch of that bottom color "up" gives you an amazingly coordinated look.

Feel the tie. Does it feel good to touch? No cheesy-feeling tie fabrics, please. Heavier silk doesn't always mean better quality, but the best ties are fully lined.

> Mistake: Wearing a dressy-looking tie with casual fabrics like khakis, denim, or cords. — JoAnna

Fabrics of more casual looking ties include wool, linen, cotton, cashmere, rayon challis, and blends of all of these. Of course, some ties in these fabrics are dressier as well. Wearing a tie with a denim shirt or other casual fabrics can be a great look for business casual—just remember that serious, silky, dressy-looking ties are for dress shirts only. Consider retro and fun patterns as well as classic patterns in these more casual fabrics.

To make sure that the two ends of your tie hang in unison, the small end gets slipped through the loop that is sewn on the back of the large end. At least one of my experts tucks the small end in between two buttons on his shirt and, according to the Prince of Wales, the reason that he can get away with this and still be considered an expert is because he knows the rules so he can break them.

When is the short end of your tie too short? When it isn't long enough to fit through the loop. If you are tall (over 6'4"), or have a large midsection that takes up tie length, and you don't want to be confined to the limited choice of extra-long ties, the loop on the back can be moved up as much as 4". A smaller knot takes up less fabric. To review your knots, go to page 100.

A bow tie—no clip-ons or pre-tied, ever—can look elegant and hip; even men who don't wear them think so. There are many ways of being stylish—if you would expect a snicker if you wear a bow tie, you may get what you expect. If you wear one because you love this style, you'll get smiles and admiring glances. Wearing one every day could become your *signature statement*.

Tie jewelry is personal preference. One of my experts likes tie tacks, including vintage; another likes tie clips and tie bars. My expert who likes tie bars/clips recommends that you not wear your tie bar too high up and that you consider placing it at an interesting slant. The slant would drive some men crazy—they are the ones who will try to straighten yours if you wear it this way. Could tie jewelry become your *signature statement*?

An ascot was, and still is, depending on the year, used to fill the bare gap at the neck when a man isn't wearing a tie. Seen mostly in old movies, it is another item that comes and goes in fashion. Some of my experts think they are pretentious, and one wears an ascot with a tweed jacket and button-down shirt because he doesn't like open necks, especially in the winter.

Some men are very sentimental about their ties—one said that ties are like old friends, you never throw them away. My experts all agree that you won't want to dry-clean your ties except as a last resort. Some have been successful with a company called Tiecrafters, Inc., in New York—men from all over the world send them their ties to clean, repair, or change the width. You can call them at 212-629-5800, write them at 252 W 29th Street, New York, New York 10001, or check their website at www.tiecrafters.com, where they offer a free brochure of tips on tie care.

Keeping your ties in good shape is important. The fabric and contour will last longer if you capsize it—take it off the same way you put it on. Loosen the knot slightly by pulling down on it, and then gently pull the wide end out. Also recommended is loosely rolling your tie up, small end first, and letting it sit that way overnight. Some lucky men have big shallow drawers where their ties stay rolled.

Since ties are a personal expression, it's sometimes difficult to wear a tie that is a gift—someone else's idea of what you should wear or what would look good on you. Feelings can be easily hurt so if you are with someone whose *taste* is different from yours, perhaps you could work it out that when it comes to ties (or all clothing), you could shop together because *you value her/his opinion*. Understand that I didn't just say that you can't buy ties for yourself when the other person isn't with you.

My experts agree that, when the gift giver is a wife, girlfriend, or child, you should wear the tie (shirt or sweater) at least once. Men usually fall into one of two camps—those who wouldn't ever make a decision without their significant other and those who would never let anyone else be involved in their attire.

The chairman of a large insurance company based in the Midwest hired me to do some wardrobe workshops for some of his employees, both men and women. He wanted me to meet with the president of the division that I would be working in and with the director of human services a couple of weeks ahead of time, so I flew in for part of a day. First I met briefly with the director, a physician with a wonderfully warm manner who was dressed in a casual suit, shirt, and a tie that didn't go with anything, giving him a bit of a rumpled professor look. He told me very nicely that he didn't believe in what I do—that it's what is *inside* a person that counts, not what they look like. I told him that I agreed with him entirely and explained that I just wanted to help people remove any visual barrier that might be keeping others from noticing their **inside**.

He was unconvinced, and we went together to meet with the president of the division, a man who was "all buttoned up," as precise and stiff as his attitude. Although his suit, shirt, and tie were coordinated with each other, they were not flattering to *him*. Somehow during our conversation the director mentioned that he didn't buy anything to wear without his wife's advice—the president, in a disdainful tone of voice, said that his wife only dared to buy him something once.

The president didn't attend any of my workshops, but the director attended all of them. Afterwards he came up to me and told me that I was fabulous and that he now realized the importance of the self-confidence that comes from knowing you look great—that when it comes to achieving the career you want, a person can get more out of life when their **outside** matches their **inside**. He even sent me a handwritten note thanking me again and saying that he and his wife had a lot of fun finding him some color-perfect ties.

> You don't have to be a trend maker, a clothes buff, or have a lot of money to look great every day. — JoAnna

SUITING UP FOR PERFECTION

JUST THE BASICS

❗ A *perfect* suit is classic in style—it is a solid-color neutral, the pieces of which (jacket and pants) can be interchanged to give you more looks.

BEYOND THE BASICS

Regardless of how casual some workplaces have become and how tired everybody is of the overworked phrase *"dress for success,"* if you want to look powerful, put on a suit even without a tie. It's better for you to have one *perfect* suit and wear it over and over than have several that are *less*.

What does the *perfect* suit look like?

! It will fit as if it was made especially for you.

! From a quality standpoint, the fabric will feel good to the touch (have a nice hand) and be well cut so that it drapes beautifully. Usually made of 100% wool, it will have good resilience (resist wrinkles) and wear well—obvious quality but not necessarily expensive to own.

! The first perfect suit you buy should (probably) be navy blue.

! The size of the lapels will neither be very narrow nor very wide.

! The jacket will be a classic, yet contemporary looking, with 2-button or 3-button styling, probably with a center vent.

! The trousers will likely be pleated and have cuffs.

! Most importantly, the perfect suit will give you the exact look you want for classic business, business casual without a tie, for interviews, and for all dressy events except formal.

Suits are always dressier looking than an odd jacket with trousers. They are the epitome of *easy elegance* because you start with two pieces that match and all you have to do is add the perfect shirt and tie.

How many suits do you need? Need, want, and can afford are different things. Advice as to the number of suits and jackets to begin your wardrobe, and which to buy first, varies from expert to expert and from industry to industry. If your industry is almost always business casual, I still recommend that you own the first two suits on my list below because you can wear them, or their components (just the jackets or trousers), to create every look you really need, short of black tie. They will work for interviews, strictly business, business casual, dressy evening, and casual evening.

If you will be wearing suits to work most every day, if you can, start with three or four and build to ten because wearing a suit only once every two weeks can triple its life. If you wear a suit once a week, it should last about five years. Meanwhile, just make sure you don't have a Monday suit—where everyone in your office can tell what day it is by what suit you are wearing. It's rumored that Charles Revson, the founder of the giant makeup company Revlon, owned 200 custom-made suits.

Some experts will tell you that you shouldn't wear a suit more than once a week because it needs to rest that long between wearings and it will last longer if you don't. Of course most things will last longer if you don't use them. If you need to, you will wear the same suit every day, with pride because you will look superb every day.

For many, finding the money to purchase any clothing is difficult, let alone several suits, but if you are one of those men who has a little extra after paying the bills and eating, and you spend first on non-business computer gadgets and other electronic gadgets like big-screen TVs, DVDs, the latest cell phone, palm-held devices, and stuff for other hobbies, please remember that investing in the way you look is an investment toward your future—so you can have as many DVDs as you want and send your kids to college.

The Best Suits

The following list of suits is for classic business. Without a tie, the solid colors are also for business casual and their components can be combined for other business casual looks. I have separated my top choices from those of other experts, only for simplicity in your reading and understanding, not to set the lists apart as good advice and bad advice. To get all of the information for this book, I only interviewed men whose advice I highly respect—we don't always see eye to eye when it comes to colors and color combinations, my specialties.

My Top Five Suits

#1 Navy blue 2- or 3-button.

#2 Dark gray 2- or 3-button.

#3 Navy or black double-breasted or black 2- or 3-button (black might be, but shouldn't be, industry-sensitive).

#4 Navy, gray, or black double-breasted or 2- or 3-button navy, gray, or black (add one in a color you didn't get above).

#5 Same as #4, adding one in a color you don't yet have or adding another in the same style that is lighter or darker in tone and/or a different texture.

Except for the first suit on the list, you can purchase the others in any order of your preference. My top five are all solid colors so you can interchange the pieces to create many interesting business casual looks. Pin-striped and chalk-striped suits are not included because they don't have this versatility which I think is necessary when you are just beginning to build a working wardrobe; however, if you are dying for one, you certainly may substitute a gray or navy stripe as you wish.

The top choices from other experts are listed in the order they are recommended to purchase—note that advice among experts differs and that some choices match mine.

Other Experts' Top Five Suits

#1 Navy blue; dark gray.

#2 Dark gray; navy; navy pin-stripe.

#3 Navy blue stripe; dark gray.

#4 Navy stripe; gray stripe; olive, tan, or taupe.

#5 Plaid; black; olive, tan, or taupe.

One expensive wardrobe book showed five suits on the cover as the best five to build your wardrobe around. Of the shirt and tie combinations shown with these suits, only one was okay from a color standpoint, and the others were bad—very bad. If even these experts can't combine colors well, how do I expect you to learn? Because I'm your teacher. Your job at this moment is to learn a new skill—read, absorb, and put your new knowledge into practice.

The Top Five Blazers and Odd Jackets

I think that it's super to use the jackets from your suits as "odd jackets," and many experts and very well dressed men agree—they are fond of saying that the two pieces that come with a suit are not glued together! However, other experts would *never* use their suits in this way. Why? Different reasons. They have so many clothes they don't need to. One part of your suit will wear out before the other—a point well taken but not necessarily true if you wear both the jacket and trousers as separates and not a reason to not utilize these pieces when you need to. If you are not willing to use your suits in this way, please add, or substitute, a navy blue blazer or jacket for one of the suits on my list. See my special notes after the list.

My Top Picks For Blazers/Sport Jackets

#1 Navy blue single-breasted blazer.

#2 Navy blue double-breasted.

#3 Black, but only if it looks good on you.

Bold and Subtle

YES   **for Muted or Gentle Coloring**   NO   **for Contrast and Light-Bright Coloring – the colors in tie are too toned-down.**

YES   **for Contrast and Light-Bright Coloring**   NO   **for Gentle and Muted coloring – colors in tie are too bright.**

Clothing and accessories courtesy of Macy's.
Photos courtesy of The Photographer's Gallery.

Bold and Subtle

YES   for Contrast or Muted Coloring

NO   for Light-Bright or Gentle Coloring
– tie is too bold and overpowering

YES   for Light-Bright or Gentle Coloring

NO   for Contrast or Muted Coloring –
color combination too blended,
quiet looking

Pattern Sizes

Large Pattern

Small Pattern

Medium Pattern

For a pulled-together look, select a tie that includes the colors of your jacket, shirt, and trousers.

#4 Camel hair—especially if your hair is blond, brown, or red, or if you have golden tones to your skin.

#5 Dark gray.

After a navy blazer, you could add the jackets above in any order you like. Just under the dressiness of a navy suit, and a great wardrobe basic, is a navy blazer with matching trousers. Blazers with brass or silver buttons are dressier looking than those with matching buttons—BUT those with matching buttons are more easily combined with a variety of casual pants, such as khakis and jeans. Also, 2- and 3-button style jackets work more easily with casual pants and jeans than those that are double-breasted.

All experts agree that your first jacket should be a navy blazer—after that their opinions vary slightly depending on the season. Consider adding a tweed, herringbone, check, or plaid jacket for the fall and winter (remember to pick patterns that compliment your Color Type) and add lighter colors for spring and summer.

SUIT YOURSELF

A woman's best accessory is a well dressed man. A boss's best asset, and worst asset, could just be his employees. The fastest way to have your talents noticed is to **look** like you know everything. — JoAnna

JUST THE BASICS

◆ Buy suits, blazers, and jackets that have a personality.

◆ Boxy and stiff looks have been replaced by softer shoulders and a slightly nipped waist.

◆ Your goal is to appear appropriate and stylish, so you will want:

★ Attitude—a good one.

★ Presence—the way you carry yourself.

★ A total look—appropriate, notable, impeccable without obsession—one of *easy elegance*.

BEYOND THE BASICS

We are experiencing a return to elegance and more formal business attire—many charming men never left this look behind. Even without *having* to, more men are choosing to wear suits while others, who used to be able to dress business casual, are being required to wear suits and ties. Clubs and restaurants whose dress codes were relaxed to accommodate the dot.com crowd (first, to no tie, and then to no jacket necessary) find that more and more men are coming in wearing suits.

Who taught you about clothing and style when you were growing up? My experts learned from their fathers, their work in the clothing industry, the movies, and the street.

Although you certainly only need to know what you like and what looks good on you, knowing the lingo of men's wardrobing can give you confidence—like cap toe; modified spread collar; full break; expect to see felt on the back of most jacket collars; and that it's fine if the buttons on your jacket sleeve are *kissing*, sewn on so close together that they touch each other.

The newest styling for suits is the shape-flattering *soft suit* (a classic look brought forward from the '30s and '40s) that has taken the place of the more shapeless sack suit as a basic in a man's wardrobe. What makes a suit a soft suit? Is it the cut? The fabric? The shoulders? Or just no stiffness in the chest area? It's all of these things. The stiffness is gone and the softness everywhere. The most apparent difference is in the more lightly padded natural shoulder. With less padding there's more room in the armhole, so these suits tend to have a comfortable fit.

With less formality, these jackets work as well with jeans, khakis, cords, and miscellaneous dress pants as well as they do with the matching suit trousers. Be aware that a highly starched shirt may look out of place with this softer silhouette—it will depend a lot on the dressiness of the fabric. When the fabric is more casual, or you want to dress the look down, choose softer shirting fabrics, and skip the starch. Always keep a good crease in the trousers.

Some suits are made to fit close to the body and some are made to drape over the body. You will find those with high-cut armholes and those with more room in this area.

Men's suit styles used to be fairly closely defined by whether they were American, British/English, or European/Italian. Each was differentiated by the number, or lack, of vents, the sharpness or softness of the shoulders, a definition at the waist, and the "drop"—the difference in measurement between your chest and your waist. Now, both vented and non-vented, waist-defined, and softer shouldered looks could come from any manufacturer or designer in any country.

The Drop

One difference is still prevalent—the drop. To accommodate differences in body shape, different manufacturers cut the same size suit with trousers that have a different waist measurement. It seems that the majority of American men still have about a 6" drop. So, if you buy an "American cut" size 40 suit, the trousers that come with it will have a 34" waist. European cuts will often have a 7" to 8" drop, so the trousers on those size 40 suits have a 32" or 33" waist. An athletic cut has an 8" to 10" drop; an executive or portly cut, a 4" drop—I guess for the executive who has been sitting at his desk too long.

Why do you need to know this? It's an issue of well fitting clothing. And because knowledge gives you power and self assurance—if you are buying your first suit and you wonder why the pants fit differently, now you'll know why. Also, those of you with a specific build may need to zero in on certain manufacturers who make the drop that is best for your body. Trousers can usually be taken in or let out about 2" at the waist, giving you more leeway, so if you have a 6" drop but want to wear a European cut, you can. Not a concern for most of you, but if pants are taken in too much, the back pockets can end up too close together.

Lapels

What is the width of the *perfect* lapel? Experts disagree. What you see in the stores varies from season to season and from style to style, but with today's *classics* it is generally 3" to 4". Usually, but not always, lapel width and the width of your tie should be about the same. I personally like lapels and ties that are in the range of 3" but appreciate all of the different varieties and love that you have a choice. From the standpoint of looking good on you, for both lapel and tie width, keep in mind your body structure. If you have a narrow build, lapels and ties that look normal on someone else will look wider on you and if you are broader, they will look narrower.

Jacket Length

Your jacket needs to be long enough to just cover your seat. The rule of "thumb" is that it should fall into your curled-up fingers when your arms are at your sides. This doesn't always work because arm lengths can vary by several inches.

Jackets are made in short, regular, long, extra-long, and longer. The only **constant** guideline for the length of a classic jacket is that it should cover your seat. The difference in the length of the torso of two 6' men could be several inches. Therefore, the following is a loose guideline just to get you started:

Short: under 5' 8"
Regular: 5' 8" to 6'
Long: 6' 1" to 6' 3"
Extra Long: 6' 4" to 6' 6"

Wearing your jackets too long can shorten your leg line. Why worry about this? Because it can make you look dumpy or frumpy, even portly, when you aren't. Stylish and dumpy are antonyms. What to do? Buy jackets in lengths that just cover your seat—for some of you, that might mean buy-ing a short instead of a regular, or a regular instead of a tall, for example. If the styling of a jacket you love is longer (you can even find some that are made to come to your knees), you can counteract the effect by making sure that your trousers are slim and tapered—not wide and/or baggy in the leg.

For the longest leg line possible, wear shoes and socks that match your trousers and have them cuffed with a medium to full break.

The 3-Piece Suit

The 3-piece suit is always dressier than the same suit would be without a vest. It is a classic look that is more popular from time to time that you can choose to wear *anytime*. Definitely pull the vests from your 3-piece suits and wear them with odd (but coordinated looking) trousers and jackets. If the vest is a stripe or a pattern, your trousers should match one of those colors. Also wear just the vest and trousers from your suits for terrific business casual looks. There are 3-piece suits that are made with a contrasting vest as well as those where the vest and trousers match but the jacket is different.

The Double-Breasted Jacket

A double-breasted jacket is always dressy looking, but it's less dressy in a blazer than a suit. Classic business colors are navy, gray, and black. When worn with matching trousers, the double-breasted jacket is dressier than when worn with contrasting trousers—black blazer with black trousers versus the same jacket with gray trousers, for example. The most classic double-breasted jacket is a 6-button. You will also see double-breasted jack-ets that have 6 buttons that roll to the bottom button (a 6-to-1), meaning it was styled for you to just button the bottom button. You will also see 2-, 4-, and 8-button jackets. It looks best worn buttoned—button the middle but-ton, leaving the bottom button open and make sure you button the anchor button on the inside so the jacket hangs evenly.

Some of the lapels on double-breasted jackets are wider and some have an upper slashing angle that flares out, making them appear wider. Wider lapels are not flattering to men with small heads or thin, long necks. Sometimes the amount of hair on the head is important—more hair/longer hair can help balance the width.

A wealthy client of mine had to buy a new tuxedo because his daughter was getting married. I met him and his wife at an expensive men's store—the owner was there to assist with the choice. The first jacket the owner selected for my client to try was a double-breasted with wide, upper slashing lapels. It fit him beautifully. Everybody, but me, was enthusias-tically telling him how fabulous it looked on him. He turned to me and asked me what I thought—all eyes were now on me.

Sensitive to the fact that everybody else loved it, I started my comment with a compliment and collaboration: *It's a very elegant tuxedo and it fits perfectly. I'm concerned that the width of the lapel is making his head look small.* Everyone turned back to look at him, and the owner was the first to say, in amazement, that it was true. My client had a thin, long neck and wore his hair very short—basically a crew cut—and wasn't interested in wearing it any other way. Based on his new knowledge, the owner of the store selected a shawl collar jacket. It was perfect—in every way. The consultation and sale were over in less than three minutes and I had a new devotee of my services—the owner.

TO VENT OR NOT TO VENT

JUST THE BASICS

   🎗 No vent, center vent, or side vents is personal preference.

   🎗 With correct fit, all styles can be flattering.

BEYOND THE BASICS

Jackets come with either a single center vent, side vents, or no vent (sometimes referred to as non-vented). Regardless, the jacket needs to fit smoothly over your seat without the vents spreading or pulling. All three styles can be flattering to all backsides if they are tailored perfectly for yours.

You will find that the majority of jackets have a center vent, but most stores that sell men's clothing will offer a choice. Several years ago, jackets with a center vent were a bit boxy (the sack), not because of the vent but because the jacket was cut fairly straight up and down. Now you will find that most suits, vented or not, will be slightly shaped (nipped in) at the waist, giving a more flattering definition.

Buttons

Suit jackets and odd jackets/blazers with matching buttons are virtually identical and either one could have three or four buttons on the sleeve (no significance). There are blazers that have matching buttons instead of metal buttons that look identical in every detail to the jacket of a suit. That means that you can utilize your suit jackets as odd jackets, including using your navy suit jacket as a blue blazer. Just so you know, one of my experts is very adamant that what makes a blazer a blazer is the metal buttons. So, if you wish, you can think about them in the same way and just consider a blazer with the matching buttons to be an odd jacket.

Pockets

Pocket flaps—straight across or slanted—are the most common and the most conservative, but they are not the dressiest. The dressy besom pocket is an opening built into the suit, and some jackets with flaps are being made so that you can tuck the flap into the pocket to give it this dressier look. The patch pocket, once only found on odd jackets, with or without a flap makes a suit look more casual. Once in a while you will find a jacket with a small second pocket on the left above the normal pocket. It's called a ticket pocket, but you can put anything in it that you want as long as it doesn't make a bulge.

The Black Suit

There seems to be some strong differing opinions on "the black suit." Some stylish men don't like it at all—others feel that it's appropriate for younger men but not for them. They think of it as very dressy and good for evening and official ceremonies (including funerals), just under the tuxedo in its formalness. But most experts feel that there is no more stigma for black suits and that every man should have at least one. Not wanting to steer you wrong, *just in case*, some of my experts are not willing to recommend it for an interview—others quickly say, "Why not?"

There are only two good reasons that I know of not to wear a black suit—if the color black doesn't look good on you and if you are going to be interviewing with a firm that might view it as too formal—one that is 24/7 strictly business casual, for example. You do want to look like you would fit right in and it's fine to be more dressed up than the person who is interviewing you—they expect it.

Even though *superstitions* have been declared finished, the black suit seems to still be a bit industry-sensitive, professional looking for more creative fields, and sometimes iffy for those that are more conservative. When in doubt, wear navy and gray, especially when it comes to interviews, until you are comfortably "in the door." Once you see what other men, especially the top men, are wearing, you can follow suit (pun intended).

BUTTON, ANTI-BUTTON, UNBUTTON ☺

JUST THE BASICS

☺ It's always safe and elegant for you to button the button closest to your waistline and leave the bottom button of your jacket or blazer open.

BEYOND THE BASICS

One of the age-old questions about a man's wardrobe is, "How many buttons should you button?" The only thing that the majority of well dressed men can agree on it that you always leave the bottom button open, and even then there are exceptions. Other than that, it seems to be strong personal preference.

2-button: Button only the top button.

3-button: Button the top two; just the middle button; or, for a more up-fashion look, just the top.

4-button: Button the middle two; the top three; or, for a more up-fashion look, just the top two.

6-button classic double-breasted: Button the middle.

6-to-1 double-breasted: Button only the bottom button—the lapel is designed to roll to the last button.

Other: You will also see a variety of other single- and double-breasted suits, jackets, and blazers with more or fewer buttons. If what to button isn't clear, ask the opinion of more than one "expert."

Some of the 3-button jackets have a higher stance (the buttons are higher), giving them a look close to that of a 4-button. I personally like men to have good looking options—for those of you who work in fields where you can be more expressive from a style standpoint, consider 4-button styles and those with a Mandarin collar. Some experts say that they are a younger look, but one of my experts, the most stylish and exquisitely dressed man I have ever met, wears both—he's in his early 50s.

All experts agree that your suits and jackets should have quality buttons, but when it comes to teaching you how to figure out if they are, it seems to come down to weight. Horn buttons, a very good choice, are heavier than plastic made to look like horn. Buttons are easily changed. Note that a two-tone horn button, versus a solid color, gives a more casual look to a suit or jacket as does a button that is a different color entirely.

Even though a lot of men don't pay any attention to matching the metals on their blazer buttons with their watch, belt buckle, shoe buckles, or cufflinks, I hope you will. If you want the coordination but not the concern of having to remember this detail, there are blazer buttons that are a combination of silver and brass that will work with everything. If it's too much work to locate a blazer with these buttons, look for the perfect blazer and then have the buttons changed. You can also choose to skip the detail by wearing a blazer that has buttons that match the color of the jacket. Overly shiny buttons look *overly* shiny.

Contrary to the opinion offered in another book, blazers with brass or silver buttons look dressier than those that have matching buttons (my experts, including those in New York, Washington, Los Angeles, and Paris, agree). The fact that they are a dressier look can keep them from working well with more casual trousers. All jackets with matching buttons (versus metal) can be combined more easily with more casual pants and jeans.

KEEP YOUR PANTS ON AND UP

JUST THE BASICS

- ♣ Wear trousers at your waist (navel), not on your hips.

- ♣ Long enough to cover the back of your shoes.

- ♣ Cuffed or plain bottom—personal preference, but cuffed is the choice of the majority and it is the style that best balances a heavier looking shoe.

- ♣ One, two, or three pleats or plain front—personal preference, but pleats are desired by the majority.

BEYOND THE BASICS

To cuff or not to cuff—it's personal preference, but cuffs are a very strong favorite. Should men who are below average in height avoid cuffs? No. Cuffs don't make you look shorter, but wearing your trousers too short can. Although there is a bit of differing opinion on cuffing plain-front pants, most experts agree that cuffs on pleated trousers are a must. Exceptions are made for more up-fashion looks.

Occasionally when you buy trousers to fit your waist, they will be too big or baggy in the seat. They can, and should, be taken in. Wearing your pants below your waist makes you look heavier, bigger in the stomach. If you wear them above your waist, you'll get the same effect—not a good one. Again, check your side view. Sometimes this is a question of vanity; you can wear the same size you always have, you just can't fasten them around your middle. Other times, it's a question of the "rise."

Trousers in the same size don't all have the same rise, the distance between the crotch and the waist, and that's convenient because men, even if they are the same height, are different. Wear trousers that are comfortable for you, but make certain they rise to your waistline. Don't know where your waist is? Generally, it's in the vicinity of your belly button. Butt cleavage is not cool—don't even think of wearing low-slung pants to work anywhere.

Single pleat, double pleats, triple pleats? Although the double pleat is *classic*, all pleated trousers serve the same purpose—comfort. The number of pleats, and which way they face (toward the pocket or toward the fly), is a matter of personal preference. The single pleat is deeper, so you have about the same amount of room as you would have with the double pleats. With triple pleats, which sometimes start at the pocket, you will generally find that the trousers are cut fuller in the upper leg—a consideration if you have thin legs or want to wear them with a jacket that is styled longer than a classic jacket.

Pleated trousers will work with all jacket styles, while those that have a plain front work better with odd jackets than they do as part of a classic suit. Normally you will want to wear pleated trousers when you are wearing a double-breasted jacket or blazer. Khakis with or without pleats? It's personal preference, with pleats out-selling the flat front.

If you are wearing pleats in any amount, the most important thing is that they hang straight and don't pull or spread open (pockets shouldn't pull or spread either). If they fit perfectly, pleated trousers can be slimming and can actually camouflage that temporary weight gain that I'm sure you don't want me to refer to as a pot, paunch, or gut.

Generally, fuller cuts and slimmer cuts are not considered classic, but we are moving into an era of acceptance and appreciation of all styles. Trousers get narrower, or taper, from below the seat. This taper helps you look broader in the shoulder and slimmer at the hip. The classic measurement at the cuff is usually about 9" across, or 18" around—depending on the manufacturer and the year, you will also find those that measure 17" or even 16".

Why do you need to know this? For a couple of reasons. If you are below average in height and you buy a pair of pants and take them to the tailor at your cleaners to be cuffed/hemmed, you need to know to ask him/her to re-taper them starting from just below your seat. If they just cut the leg off, they are cutting off some of the taper and you can end up with a dowdy, shorter legged look. The second reason is for all men who might want to wear a longer jacket or for those of you who have short legs and a long torso. Longer jackets can definitely make your legs look shorter, so if the jacket is longer than just covering your seat, you will want to make sure that your trousers are tapered to less than the classic 18".

How to tell if your legs are short in comparison to your body? Maybe you've noticed that your in-seam measurement is less than that of a friend who is about your height. If he wears a 34/34 and you wear a 34/30, that's a clue. Also, look in the mirror and you will be able to tell if your torso appears long in comparison to your legs.

Most all men, even men who don't own a suit, have a pair of gray flannel or gray wool trousers—they seem to say, "I'm dressed up now," in a very quiet way. When you are going to buy a new pair, think about whether a dark, medium, or light gray will best flatter your coloring when it comes to coordinating them with your blazers and odd jackets.

Lighter and medium grays make a nice contrast with a navy or black blazer and also work well with camel, dark gray, and other odd jackets that have at least a touch of gray. When it comes to wearing gray trousers with gray jackets, please make sure that the grays are from the same color family—just lighter/darker versions of the same shade of gray. A reminder: The most flattering grays do not have a brownish or muddy cast.

I asked my experts if they would ever wear plaid trousers from one their suits (they all own at least one plaid suit) with a sweater for a casual look. One of them said, "Not knowingly or willingly." One said, "Never!" But others said, "Why not? The pieces of a suit don't come glued together." I personally love using my suits in this way—you already know where I stand. The point is not for you to own plaid trousers or a plaid suit, but to encourage you to pull your suits apart and utilize the pieces as you like because it can double your wardrobe.

⊘   **Bad Advice:** Wear a black turtleneck sweater with plaid trousers that don't have any black in them.

⊕   **My Advice:** To make this look work, the color of your sweater or shirt needs to match one of the apparent colors (highly visible) in the trousers.

Microfibers are being used for pants—both high end and low end—that might still feel like the old polyester knits. More up-fashion styles that have a good hand, and perhaps a good look, may be hot to wear (no, not that *hot*, the hot you feel when you perspire). Synthetics don't breathe (let the air through), so even a light-weight wool could be cooler than a microfiber.

Trousers last longer when they are lined, and most wool pants come lined to the knee. Some men are requesting that they be totally lined so the wool isn't itchy.

You can wear "winter white," cream, and beige pants year round. It's what you choose to wear **with** them that will make the difference in looking appropriate for each season. Business casual looks are easily created with these colors if you wear them with a matching shirt or sweater making a *base* to top with blazers and jackets in both solid colors like gray, navy, black, and brown, as well as with tweeds, plaids, herringbones, or checks that contain a touch of cream or beige. If you like, add a tie that has a touch of your base and jacket colors.

Keep color balance in mind. If you are wearing light pants, like stone or sand (a light whitish-gray) khakis, for example, and a black shirt or sweater, wear black shoes and belt to pull the look together. Even better, add a coordinating jacket that combines light gray (to emulate the stone/sand) and black.

WHITE OUT

JUST THE BASICS

⚓   No matter how expensive it is, a pure white shirt will look cheap on about 50% of you.

♣ If pure white makes you look pale, pops off your skin, or looks inexpensive on you, simply wear *soft white*—it will actually still look like white on **you**.

BEYOND THE BASICS

I hate the word *cheap,* but I'm using it because, in this instance, it is so descriptive that I know you'll pay extra close attention to what follows. What am I talking about? As strange as it may seem, only 50% of you are flattered by **pure** white. Use your mirror test.

If pure white tends to jump off your skin and look visually too bright, or inexpensive (cheap), you can still look good in clean looking softer whites, off-whites, creams, winter white, and beige (ecru). Clean looking? Sometimes these shades can have a brownish oatmeal, grayish, putty, or taupe cast—*please* avoid these. And, unless your skin tone is golden, avoid yellowish looking whites, yellowish looking off-whites, yellowish looking creams, and yellowish looking ecrus/beiges.

Did I just tell some of you that you can't wear the business icon—the white shirt? No, I said that 50% of you will look better in *less bright* whites, specifically those of you who have Gentle or Muted coloring. A soft white will look white on **you**, not "cheap."

☐ Which Color Types are enhanced by pure white?

☐ Contrast Color Types can wear pure white head-to-toe.

☐ Light-Bright Color Types can do the same.

☐ Gentle Color Types can wear a small amount of pure white in a print or as a trim. Soft whites will still look like white on you.

☐ Muted Color Types should avoid pure white in any amount. Soft whites will look like white on you.

> It is a mistake to think that you can wear a white shirt with just any suit or tie. — JoAnna

White shirts do not look great, or even good, with some suits and some ties. Blended looking fabrics like nailsheads, houndstooths, and muted-looking plaids are generally not complimentary with a pure white, or possibly even soft white, shirt, as the shirt can make the suit look dirty or drab by comparison. If you see this happening, use a cream or beige/ecru shirt.

Any tie, regardless of whether it contains clear or toned down colors, that has soft white/cream/beige/ecru in it will not look good on a pure white shirt. Ties that contain only clear colors look wonderful on a pure white, but ties in toned down, muted colors do not, so it's best to wear them with cream/beige/ecru shirts.

Avoid wearing a white or soft white shirt with a cream or beige/tan jacket unless the tie has both the white and cream or beige in it, for the same reason as above. Substitute cream or beige/ecru and note how much more expensive both the shirt and jacket look. A white shirt generally works well with a light colored khaki/chino often called sand or stone.

How can you see for yourself the difference between pure white and softer whites?

In a men's clothing department, find, pick up, and carry around with you a shirt that you are certain is a pure, bright white. How to tell? Actually "touch it" to other shirts to make sure you have the whitest shirt in the place. While you are comparing it, you will automatically find shirts that are a "softer" white.

Since everyone can wear the softer whites, what you want to do is to find out if you can ALSO wear a pure white. Go to a mirror, hold it up, and see if it "pops out," looks overly bright and inexpensive on you or if you are holding your own and you look healthy. Then hold up the soft white—you will like it because it looks good on all Color Types—hold up the pure white again and see if **it** likes you as well. Think *equal to*, just a different effect.

KEEP YOUR SHIRT ON

JUST THE BASICS

- ▲ A white shirt is not always a safe choice.

- ▲ Impeccably pressed.

- ▲ 100% cotton or high percentage of cotton with small percentage of "other."

- ▲ Button-downs are casual and should not be worn with dressy suits, blazers, or ties.

- ▲ Classic straight point and modified spread collars go with all suit, jacket, and blazer styles, face shapes, and neck lengths/widths.

- ▲ Avoid wide spread/extreme spread and long pointed collars.

- ▲ Not too big or too tight in the neck.

- ▲ Not more than ½" cuff showing.

- ▲ Collar points touch the body of your shirt when wearing a tie.

- ▲ You don't have to wear an undershirt unless you need to.

- ▲ No "ring around the collar."

BEYOND THE BASICS

If you ever work without your jacket on, your dress shirt becomes even more important.

There is no such thing as a short-sleeved dress shirt—they aren't made so therefore you can't wear one. Well, maybe I just lied, but not about your wearing one, EVER! No, not even with a tie—especially not with a tie! **All** short-sleeved shirts are casual shirts.

When the technology is perfected, you can wear a no-iron shirt as long as it looks as good as an impeccably ironed 100% cotton shirt.

What is your perfect shirt sleeve length? Your jacket sleeve should cover your wrist bone and fall just to the bottom of the indentation where your thumb and your wrist join. The cuff of a long-sleeved shirt will hang just below that and it's personal preference how much cuff you show—somewhere between ¼" and ½", but I advise never more than ½". You definitely don't want the button on your shirt cuff, or your cufflinks, to show when you are standing with your arms by your side.

The trick is to get your jacket sleeve long enough so you still look elegant when you aren't wearing a long-sleeved shirt, but not so long that when you show some cuff the overall effect is too long.

Shirts are made with a variety of collar styles and cuffs in both common and exact sleeve lengths. The range in common sleeve lengths, like 33/34, may work for you, or not. Those that have two horizontal buttons on the cuff (versus one button or two vertical buttons) allow you to tighten or loosen the cuff which helps keep the sleeve length where you need it. With a French cuff shirt you don't have this advantage, so it's best to wear your true sleeve length unless the common length works perfectly for you.

On the back of the shirt across the shoulders you will find either a box pleat in the center or pleats on the sides. Some men find a difference in range of movement, while others feel that they are equally comfortable. The same goes for pleats, rather than gathers, where the cuff and sleeve are joined. If a sleeve is just tapered to the cuff without either pleats or gathers (this shirt is less expensive to make), movement is more confined.

Better shirts will have a button on the sleeve placket (the opening above the cuff). Called a gauntlet button, it should be kept closed.

Most men prefer that the body of their shirts have a regular cut versus one that is tapered, because they like the ease of movement. It's personal preference and if you are on the thin side you may favor those that are slightly tapered. Skin-tight and/or pulling between buttons is neither appropriate nor elegant.

Most custom-made shirts are generally now what's called *made to measure*. You get to select the collar style, sleeve, and cuff style, and the body style. The shirt factory has each of those pieces already cut in certain sizes, and they put them together the way you like them. A reminder: Any collar or cuff that is oversized or undersized is not classic.

Eventually you will want at least 12 shirts (including two that have never been taken out of the package) that are in good shape (no stains, frays, chipped buttons) so you don't have to go to the laundry more than once a week. If you are on a budget and just starting out, start with six, plus two. Don't wear a shirt twice without laundering it, unless you only wore it for a couple of hours the first time and you swear there isn't even a hint of lingering odor.

Always include one shirt that matches each of your trouser colors—it can be slightly lighter or a hint darker. Why? Because each makes a *base*, which makes it easy for you to extend your wardrobe by wearing them with other suit jackets and odd jackets/blazers, sweaters, and vests.

Your Best Collar Styles

What styles of collars will look best on you and with your suits, jackets/blazers, and what are the most compatible knots you can tie for each? Some of the following move in and out of favor, so, depending on their current status, they will be readily available or custom order only.

◆ **Modified spread collar:** This collar has a slight spread. All knots; all suits, blazers, and jackets; all face shapes and necks. Particularly good with a double-breasted jacket.

◆ **Classic straight collar:** All knots except the full Windsor; all suits, blazers, and jackets; all face shapes and necks.

◆ **Button-down collar:** All knots except full Windsor; never with a double-breasted and best with more casual suits and jackets; all face shapes and necks. I personally like, as do some of my experts, to see this style worn with the buttons unbuttoned for business casual looks when you are wearing it without a tie—however, this look will probably raise a few eyebrows if you wear it this way for classic business casual.

◆ **Hidden button-down:** Same as above but it's dressier than a button-down so it can be worn with dressier suits.

◆ **Contrast collar:** Full Windsor may look overdone; wear with dressy suits and blazers; all face shapes and necks. Looks particularly coordinated when your tie colors include a touch of white. Most have contrasting cuffs, and many come with French cuffs. They are considered stylish by some, and slightly overdone or slightly flashy by others. I know elegant men who like them and elegant men who don't.

◆ **Tab collar, button, or snap:** All knots except full Windsor; all suits, blazers, and jackets; all face shapes and necks.

- **Pin spread collar:** All knots except full Windsor; dressy-looking suits and blazers; all face shapes and necks.

- **English eyelet:** Holes in collar for pin; all knots except full Windsor; best with dressy-looking suits and blazers; all face shapes and necks. Generally custom-made.

- **Contrast club:** Collar is rounded; all knots except full Windsor; dressy suits and blazers; all face shapes and necks except for very round faces with jowls. Custom-made.

⊘ **Bad Advice:** Long straight pointed collars go with all face shapes and jacket styles.

① **My Advice:** This collar isn't flattering to anyone.

- **Long straight point collar:** Not recommended by me for any face shape (even round) or neck size/length. Instead of lengthening a round or square face, this collar can make them look even more so by its stark contrast in shape. It also isn't helpful if your neck is short or nearly non-existent for the same reason (picture those long points starting right up under someone's chin and you'll know what I mean).

- **Wide spread collar/extreme spread/cutaway spread:** Not recommended by me for any face shape or neck size/length. Hmm, what's the best way to tell you that it looks ridiculous? It looks ridiculous. It makes a narrow or long face and long or skinny neck look more so again by stark contrast in shape. At the same time, it calls attention to a round or square face and/or short neck. And, it makes the tie look like a noose around your neck. Don't believe me? Try it on and see for yourself or just be observant when you see someone wearing it.

- **Banded collar:** Sometime referred to as collar band shirts, they work well with all face shapes and necks—strictly business casual, they can be worn with many jackets but not with a double-breasted.

Yes, I'm aware that I don't favor the full Windsor knot with many collar styles—it has to do with how much space the collar allows to accommodate this large knot. You might be able to use it with styles other than the modified spread collar if your tie is very light-weight silk.

The points of your collar should always touch the body of your shirt, and overly thick tie material and/or too large a knot can make them lift. So regardless of the guidelines above, if they don't touch your shirt, tie a smaller (or maybe just tighter) knot or choose a tie in a lighter weight silk.

Shirts are made with some variety of collar heights—they vary so that men, regardless of their neck length, can be comfortable and not have too much or too little collar showing in the back. Avoid extremes and be aware that a higher than normal collar, considered more formal by some, can make an average neck appear shorter, and a long neck look as if you are trying to camouflage it (neither is desirable), while possibly making your shoulder line look more sloping (not a good thing).

There shouldn't be puckers between double rows of stitching on the collar or elsewhere on the shirt. Some shirts are being made with a top fused collar (no rows of stitching), creating a very smooth look.

Many men wear shirts that are too tight in the collar—I have read that this can supposedly decrease your vision. The good news is that it comes back when you aren't strangling yourself. Even if you have been measured perfectly, shirts can, and often do, shrink. Generally, buy a collar size that is ½" more than you measure. Some of my experts advise that you should return any shirt that shrinks. If you buy that brand again, buy it one size larger in the neck and sleeve. You want to always have a perfect fit and not an "I'm being strangled by my shirt" look or an "I've lost weight and I'm still wearing my old shirts" look. You should be able to insert your little finger between the buttoned collar and your neck.

The Fabrics

The higher the percentage of cotton, the more readily the fabric can breathe, absorb perspiration, and survive the laundry. First choice is 100% cotton. Second choice is almost all cotton with a small percentage of another fabric.

The dressiest of the shirt fabrics are Egyptian cotton and sea island cotton. The pima cottons are also wonderful, though not quite as fine a weave. Do you really need to know about dressy shirt fabrics and more casual shirt fabrics? Some of you will, and, for the rest of you, it's important that you not wear the most casual fabrics with very dressy-looking ties or when your intent with a dressy suit is to make it look as business *formal*, or dressy evening (short of black tie) as possible. Fabrics first on the list below are generally more casual, moving down to the dressiest Egyptian and sea island cottons.

Chambray
Oxford
Pinpoint oxford
Herringbone
Royal oxford—Queen's oxford
End-on-end
Broadcloth
Polished cotton
Pima

Sea island
Egyptian

There are some extraordinary white-on-white weaves, as in a herring-bone for example, that are very dressy looking and a good expression of simple elegance with a personality.

Remember that you can wear a shirt made from a more casual shirting fabric, such as oxford cloth, to dress down a dressy suit but you will need to wear a less dressy tie as well.

Smart Shirt Details

You can never go wrong by keeping it **simple**. Please don't mistake simple for boring. Think simple, *easy elegance*, and let the cut and color of your clothing do the work. The most elegant, and often the dressiest, looks con-sist of just two colors or three colors. An example of a two-color look is a dark gray suit with a white or soft white shirt and a tie that mixes white and gray. In a three-color look, the jacket, shirt, and trousers will be different colors, and the best tie would include all three.

⊘ **Bad Advice:** Powder blue, light green, and other muted soft shades in dress shirts show you are a team player.

Ⓢ **My Advice:** 50% of you will just look ineffective and perhaps ill because toned down, quiet colors will make your skin tone look muddy, gray, or sallow. Remember to wear shirts in your best colors and clarity.

Even though there are some very dressy-looking stripes and patterns in shirt fabrics, a white or soft white shirt will always look dressier. But please remember two things: White shirts do not look good with all suit and jacket fabric weaves or all ties, and a white button-down is casual—you will see a lot of men wearing it with dressy suits and ties, but that doesn't mean they look as elegant as they should...or could.

Please don't wear a striped shirt (or other pattern) that has white in it (like a blue and white stripe) with a cream, beige, camel, or tan suit, jacket, or trousers. The shirt will look out of place and the other garments could look dirty by comparison. Exception: If your tie has both the white and the camel, for example, as well as the other color(s) in your shirt, jacket, and trousers, the look will work.

When wearing a striped shirt, make sure that at least one of the colors is repeated in the suit and tie—a lighter version of one of the colors could also work—i.e., a blue and white stripe works best with a navy suit because the blue stripe is a lighter version of the navy; a gray and white stripe is wonderful, of course, with a gray suit. Could you wear your gray and white striped shirt with your navy suit? Yes, but only if your tie combines blue and gray (for your very best look, the tie would also have a touch of white).

There are so many different kinds of stripes and patterns (like candy, awning, multi and pencil stripes, plaids, and tattersall and gingham checks) and you don't have to know what they are called because no one will ever test you on them. In addition to the classics, you can find varied color combinations such as beige and brown, gold and white, and mixes of purples. In fact, someone did a study and found that after blue, men like purple, and manufacturers/designers have picked up on information like this.

Rather than risk doing it awkwardly or very badly, don't try to combine any striped or patterned shirts with tweed, plaid, nailhead, birds eye, or any other patterned suits or jackets. You can even keep everything—suit, shirt, and tie—in solid colors until you are sure, absolutely sure, that you have created a million-dollar look (a **boardroom** look instead of a backroom look).

Choose shirts you like that flatter your coloring, then carefully coordinate them with your suits, jackets, trousers, and ties. Sound too complicated? Help on "how to do it well" is on its way, but just relax. You never have to wear a striped or patterned shirt unless you want to. If you need a change that's easier to manage from a coordination standpoint, buy some shirts in solid colors that you have never worn before—looking over your favorite ties will give you a clue as to which colors will be easiest to work into your current wardrobe. With a shirt in a color versus white or blue, all of a sudden, even your ties will look different.

Blended looking stripes and patterns (where the colors seem to run together) are not complimentary to Contrast or Light-Bright Color Types—those that are bold, bright, or have high-contrast will overpower those of you with Gentle and Muted coloring. No larger stripes for Light-Bright or Gentle Color Types. Large stripes that will work for Muted coloring will be very blended looking. This information applies not only to your shirts but to your ties, suits, and odd jackets as well.

On a quality shirt, patterns will match (line up) everywhere—particularly check the pocket to make sure the stripe/pattern aligns with that in the body of the shirt.

Find the best laundry in town (by asking neighbors, co-workers, men's stores). Expect that sometimes shirts won't survive even the best. Take the time to look over your shirts when you pick them up so you can have them redone if necessary (don't accept wrinkled collars, cuffs, or fronts).

It's a terrible feeling to be down to your last clean shirt, and that as you go to put it on, you see that a wrinkle has been firmly ironed into the collar. If you wear it you will feel self-conscious all day. So, because you cannot afford to make a bad impression, NOW is when you reach for one of the two extra shirts which you have that you have never taken out of the package—the other extra shirt is in your office in case you spill your morning coffee or have something for lunch that refuses to stay on your fork. Replace the shirt you took out of the package IMMEDIATELY.

Can you wear French cuffs with a blazer or odd jacket? My experts have differing opinions on wearing them with a blazer, but all agree that this dressy look should not be done with an odd jacket. They are wonderful with a double-breasted blazer—this is a dressy look that works much better with dress trousers versus khakis.

Quality dress shirts come with and without a pocket, but never with two pockets—shirts with two pockets are casual regardless of the fabric. Any pocket with a button is casual. One pocket or none is personal preference, but most men put one to good use—but not for leaking pens!

Buttons and/or flaps on pockets (with or without a tie) convey business casual. These shirts are gaining in popularity because men have discovered that buttons on pockets keep their handheld computer and phone from falling out when they bend over. Quality buttons are important because if they aren't, replacing those that get chipped will become a necessary "hobby." Some manufacturers are now using *unbreakable* buttons.

Quality also means that pockets will be sewn on straight and buttons will be secure. Even good garments may have a dangling thread from time to time (but never several), so you will want to look for them on every new garment you purchase and trim them (carefully). If you are seen with dangling threads, it could signify (perhaps rightly or wrongly) that you are a person who is *unaware*.

Be aware of the color of the buttons on button-down shirts, like gray buttons on blue and even white on blue, as they can interfere with your well planned color scheme. They add another detail that you have to consider. Though button-downs are never dressy, those that have matching buttons, like gray on gray, look dressier. You will find that when your tie has a touch of the color of the buttons, you will have a more coordinated look.

When wearing a shirt with a collar under a sweater or jacket without a tie, there is an age old debate about whether the collar should be worn "in or out." It's a matter of personal preference, with most conservative men generally wearing their collars "in" and those that are a touch more uninhibited utilizing both—an option I encourage, although not with wide spread collars.

Do you always have to wear an undershirt with a dress shirt? Some of my experts say, "Never!" And some say, "Always!" If you tend to perspire a lot, they do make your shirts last longer because the undershirt will take the brunt of the dampness and keep the mix of deodorant and sweat away from your shirt (the cause of staining under the arms). On the other hand, they add another layer which can make some men, who wouldn't normally perspire so much, just too hot. You get to decide, but, if you wear one, it should never, ever show above your shirt or sweater, and the sleeve shouldn't show through the fabric of your dress shirt sleeve.

To monogram or not to monogram. More differing opinions from my elegant experts. For some, no, it's too showy. For others, yes, but not on the cuff. Their preference is on the pocket or in that location on a non-pocket shirt. That way, no one sees the monogram unless you want them to—when you take your jacket off.

TIED IN KNOTS

JUST THE BASICS

- ♟ Avoid wearing silky dressy ties with casual suits or jackets.

- ♟ Choose your best pattern size and most flattering shades and clarity of colors.

- ♟ Heavier silk doesn't always mean better quality.

- ♟ No stains.

- ♟ Choose colors that look outstanding on you **and** with your suits, jackets, shirts, and trousers.

- ♟ Use a knot that works well with your collar style.

- ♟ The point of your tie ends between the top and bottom of your waistband/belt buckle.

BEYOND THE BASICS

Your ties are a personal expression—they show your personality and how much you know (or don't understand) about dressing well. Since they also communicate your mood, decorum, diplomacy, and judgment, you can use your ties (as well as your suits, jackets, and shirts) as a communication device. A husband and wife were in a cafe having lunch. A stranger approached them and, speaking directly to the wife, not even acknowledging the husband, he said, "Where did you get his tie?" Maybe this tie communicated that this particular husband wouldn't have been clever enough to choose it on his own.

I cannot impress upon on you enough your tie's importance to the way you look, and, unfortunately, they are the most difficult part of your wardrobe to get right.

> A well-tied tie is man's first serious step in life. —Oscar Wilde

The length of your tie will be perfect for you if you tie it so that the point ends no longer than the bottom of your belt buckle/waistband and no higher than the top. This is assuming, like all elegant men, that you are wearing your trousers at your waist, in the neighborhood of your navel.

The tie should hang straight and lie flat with no wrinkles or bubbles. Check it carefully because it will never look better than it does to begin with.

Knot Styles

◆ **Four-in-hand:** ties the smallest knot.

◆ **Windsor, also called the full Windsor:** the largest knot.

◆ **Half-Windsor:** medium-size knot.

◆ **Bow tie:** no clip-ons or pre-tied, **ever**.

The knot you tie will depend on your collar style. Given that, how large a knot actually turns out to be depends on the fabric of your tie—lighter weight silk versus heavier silk, knits, wovens, wool, or linen, for example. For the classic straight collar shirt I have suggested that you not use a full Windsor, but if your tie is made out of a very light silk, it might work. In general, if your face is quite small or your neck is short, you will want to avoid tying your ties in a full Windsor knot.

One of the biggest and most often made mistakes is wearing just any tie on a white shirt. It's like women and black shoes—they just don't go with everything.

> The *perfect* tie will always have at least a touch, or more, of your suit, jacket, trousers, and shirt color. — JoAnna

The best way to find a tie that will work well with a white shirt is to buy a tie that has a touch of white (or a light silver) in it. If the tie has a soft white, instead of a pure white, it will look better on a soft white shirt. If your shirt is cream, or beige/ecru and you wear a tie that has white in it, your shirt will look dirty or drab by comparison—you get the idea.

What about wearing ties that don't have white, cream, or beige/ecru in them with shirts that are white, cream, or beige/ecru? Clear colors work well with white and soft white shirts, and toned down colors are super on creams and beiges. Avoid wearing any tie that has quiet, muted, toned down colors with a bright, pure white shirt. Along the same lines, if you want to wear bright ties with a beige or ecru shirt, check them with a white shirt to see if they look better.

Generally, for classic attire, the width of the tie will approximate the width of your lapel. Most men like their ties and lapels in the middle, neither too narrow nor too wide, measuring about 3 ½". Any tie wider than 4" or narrower than 3" is likely to be either up-fashion or old-fashioned, depending on the year. Remember that a narrower tie will look narrower yet on a husky build and a wide tie always looks wider on a slender build.

VESTED INTEREST

JUST THE BASICS

♦ Leave the last button undone.

♦ Long enough in the front to cover your shirt, tie, and waistband.

♦ Borrow from your 3-piece suits and collect odd vests.

♦ An interesting layering piece for classic business casual as well as casual business looks.

♦ Wear open or closed for casual business and creative casual looks.

BEYOND THE BASICS

Vests are classic garments that get moved to the forefront of fashion from time to time. Regardless what year it is, because they are classic, you can appropriately enjoy wearing them any time you like—they could even become your *signature*.

They can be worn with most jacket and suit styles except double-breasted and blazers. When wearing a vest (buttoned) you can leave your jacket open if you prefer. With a 3-piece suit, It should fit closely to the body but not snugly or pulling at the buttons. Men tell me that it's a good sensation to *feel* the vest. More casual styles do not have to fit as closely.

Don't forget to utilize those vests that are part of your 3-piece suits. Wear just the vest and the matching trousers for any business casual look, or, for more relaxed attire, combine them with casual pants and jeans. A vest that matches your trousers can be slimming, but that doesn't mean that fuller figured men shouldn't also wear contrasting vests—strive to look exceptional, not skinnier.

For business casual, couple vests with casual shirts, including banded collar shirts, T-shirts, and sweaters. Try leather, suede, and sweater vest options. Dress shirts can also do double duty—consider a blue and white striped shirt with navy trousers (or nice dark blue jeans) and a white vest, worn open or closed. Roll up your shirt sleeves if you like.

Manmade fleece and quilted vests are extremely casual and might be acceptable for business casual on days when the temperature dips below zero and you are a hero for having made it in to the office at all.

Pullover sweater vests, a sweater without sleeves, or a sweater vest with buttons (picture a sleeveless cardigan) can be a good layering piece. Wear it with or without a tie and with or without a jacket, keeping a jacket handy when necessary. A casual vest calls for a more casual tie.

Vests in warmer months? Usually only in the movies, but there isn't anything wrong with wearing a linen or other summery looking fabric when it's hot outside—it looks *cooler* (less warm) when it's worn open.

TOP TIPS FOR *SMART* TOPS

JUST THE BASICS

- Collect interesting shirts and sweaters in your best colors to wear with your suits, blazers, jackets, and trousers.

- No T-shirts with words or pictures—small discreet logos only.

- No T-shirts that look like undershirts.

- No undershirts showing at the neck.

- Nothing stretched out, faded, or sloppy looking.

BEYOND THE BASICS

For variety, add patterned sweaters or shirts that have some of the colors of your trousers, such as a gray, blue, and black merino wool sweater to wear with both black and gray trousers. If you like, layer a sweater like this over a shirt that matches your trousers or one of the highly visible colors in the sweater. A nice plaid shirt that has a touch of navy will work well with your navy suit, navy trousers, or dark blue jeans.

When wearing a jacket with a shirt that has pockets, it's best if the edge of the pocket doesn't show at the lapel of the jacket.

Some knit shirts and sweaters eventually "grow," shrink, or bag and sag out of shape, ruining the look of an otherwise super outfit. Any garment that does this, or even starts to look worn or faded, should be given up right away. No, don't risk even one more wearing just because it happens to be clean. If you do, this will surely be the day that you are invited to sit in on a meeting that could change your life!

From the standpoint of fitting you well, check the shoulder seam in shirts and sweaters—if it falls off the shoulder down on your arm, it can give you a drooping or sloped shoulder look (especially important for men with sloping shoulders).

Casual shirts and sweaters come in a variety of wonderful fabrics and different weaves, not just good-looking cottons. You'll find light-weight merino wool, light-weight cashmere (2-ply cashmeres fit well under jackets), silk (knits, not the thin silk shirts that look a bit feminine, too flowing), blends of cotton and cashmere, rayon, and so on. Some of the mercerized cottons feel like silk.

How many buttons on your shirt can you leave open for business casual? Many casual shirts look outstanding buttoned up all the way, particularly when worn with a suit. It's safe to open the collar button and the one below. Please don't let an undershirt show (I know that I'm repeating myself).

An undershirt is not the same as a T-shirt—If it shows, it should be a *real* T. What's the difference and how could someone tell? By the apparent quality of the fabric and the feel. Think of it as a *layering piece* instead of a typical T-shirt. Picture a nice thinner fabric crewneck sweater with short sleeves (or long) in brushed mercerized cotton, silk, rayon, and blends of those. No T-shirts with your favorite sayings, sport teams, or souvenirs from your latest trip. Brand logos need to be very small and subtle. — JoAnna

---

The quality of all of your shirts and sweaters should be good—that doesn't have to dictate a high price. You can buy very nice quality for as little as $15 in the outlets or discount stores.

Wearing a cardigan with a shirt and, with or without, a tie, can add variety to your business casual looks but, please, no blousing styles—it needs to hang straight up and down and it can't do this if the ribbing on the bottom is tighter than the body of the sweater. Cardigans are classic garments that come and go in fashion, but no matter how popular they may be at any given time, they will always have much less visual presence than a jacket, so for that unforeseen meeting keep your jacket handy.

It's best not to wear the classic V-neck sweater without anything under it even if you don't have a hairy chest. Wear it over a shirt, with or without a tie, a T-shirt (as long as it doesn't look like an undershirt—I know, you got it), or over a turtleneck, with or without a jacket. By the way, whenever I refer to a turtleneck, you can substitute a mock turtleneck. The high V-neck T-shirts and sweaters are fine without anything under them.

Do men really buy and wear colors in dress shirts, casual shirts, and sweaters in other than blue, or are colors in a man's wardrobe the influence of a woman? One of my experts said, "If a man wears a color, it's usually a gift—a bad gift." Another buys for *himself* shirts in purple, pink, yellow, etc. Both men dress very well—they just have a different opinion when it comes to color.

Years ago, Bill Cosby popularized patterned sweaters for men. Some of you wear them because you like them and some of you feel encouraged to wear them because they were gifts from your significant other. Keep your best colors, clarities, and pattern sizes in mind, and, just like you would color-coordinate a tie with your suit, jacket, shirt, and trousers, make sure the colors of your trousers and shirt are in your sweater.

For ideas on well balanced looks using solid-color shirts, sweaters, and trousers, review the information on page 125.

You can tuck thinner sweaters into your trousers and jeans, or wear them out—it's personal preference—but thicker sweaters are always worn out. How will you know if it's too thick to tuck in? When you are in the process and it feels like there is too much fabric to stuff in your pants.

Many shirts come with buttons that don't match the fabric. If you are wearing a tie, the buttons don't show, but when you aren't, they do. It's always dressier looking if the buttons match, or blend very well.

Wearing two collared shirts together as a layered effect can create a creative casual look, but I would avoid wearing this particular combination for classic business casual.

There are some shirts that have lapel-like collars and they come in everything from beautifully embroidered solids to wild Hawaiian prints. In short- and long-sleeved styles, some are made to wear out, but you could also tuck those in. In this country, versus the Philippines, for example, where a beautiful shirt that is worn on the outside takes the place of a jacket, wearing your shirt out gives a completely different appearance—one that is more casual. There are some super looking prints that you can wear in this way if you work in a casual or more up-fashion atmosphere, but please make sure that the shirts you choose to wear this way are finished on the bottom versus looking like your shirt tails are hanging out.

In sweaters as in suiting fabrics, be aware that blended looks, such as heather, are generally not flattering to Light-Bright and Contrast Color Types. All Color Types should avoid wearing black shirts/sweaters with navy trousers or dark blue jeans unless you are wearing a jacket that combines both colors—even then, depending on your coloring, you will want to brighten or lighten this look.

DATABASE

JUST THE BASICS

- Wearing a shirt or sweater that matches your trousers is an *easy, elegant* way to look great—I call this combination a *base*.

- Layer a *base* with jackets you borrow from a suit, odd jackets, vests, and sweaters.

BEYOND THE BASICS

The most easy and elegant way to dress when you aren't in a suit (or don't have to wear one) is to wear a base. What's a base? It is an all one-color look that is created by wearing a shirt, nice T-shirt, sweater, or turtleneck in the **same** color as your trousers—you'll want to have as many as you can.

How closely do the colors have to match? They can be a hint lighter or darker, but they need to be close enough so that at a glance they look alike.

Having several *smart bases* allows you to have a s*mart wardrobe*—it's **by far** the easiest way in the world to look well-coordinated and elegant for business casual and other occasions where you want to look sharp but don't want to wear a tie.

You can change the look of your *smart base* simply by what you choose to wear on top of it:

- Different solid colors and styles of jackets.

- Other odd jackets like plaids, herringbones, checks, and tweeds that have the color of the base in them.

- Vests.

- Sweaters.

- Cardigans.

- Another shirt worn as a layering piece.

- Different belts and shoes.

Keeping your best color combinations in mind, the top and bottom that create your base should be both fairly **basic** and, generally, **classic**. Basic because they can be easily combined with so many other garments, and classic because you can wear them for many years. Just a change of a jacket style or accessories can instantly update classic bases, keeping them stylish.

Collect bases for work and play in all the different fabrics and colors you like. Try gray flannels with a gray merino wool turtleneck. In the spring, wear a camel mercerized cotton, silk, or rayon high V-neck pullover with tropical-weight camel trousers or khakis; even linen with linen, denim with denim, and so on.

For an *easy, elegant* look, wear bases with shoes and belts in your **hair color** (yes, your hair color—much more about this concept later) and count the compliments. Don't panic—you can always wear the classic black or brown. Because they look so pulled together, you will always look more dressed up in a base, even in denim, than you do in unmatched separates.

DON'T BELT IT DOWN

JUST THE BASICS

- Your belt belongs at your waist—not below.

- Match your shoes.

- Solid color.

- Smooth, finely textured leather for classic business.

♣ Plain but nicely finished buckle for classic business and classic business casual.

♣ No belts with braces.

♣ About 1 ¼" to 1 ½"—approximately the width of trouser cuff is classic—wider belts are best kept for business casual.

BEYOND THE BASICS

Do your shoes and belt *really* have to match? It's really an *easy, elegant* way to tie your look together, and most of the time the answer is that you will want your belt to match, or be closely coordinated with, your shoes. With the onslaught of business casual, some men feel that the rule has relaxed a little. Break it only if you can say, "equal to or better than." How to break it? You could match your belt to your pants and your shoes to your jacket. The point is that both need to relate to what you are wearing.

If you are wearing braces, you won't be wearing a belt. Otherwise, if your pants have belt loops, you will. There are a few trousers made without loops—the front closure is sometimes called a dress extension or tab, although there are trousers that have an extension that also have belt loops. I'm sure that's more than you ever wanted to know, but I know that knowledge will give you confidence and I don't want you worried about whether to belt or not.

Buy belts about 1" larger than your natural waist measurement—not what you wish it was. So, if your waist measures 35", buy 36" belts. Try them on and make sure you can easily buckle the belt in the center hole. Buckling in the center (generally the third) hole looks the most elegant. The other holes can be used if you tend to expand around your waist during the day. If you are constantly using the first hole, go up one size.

Texture, especially those that look rough, makes a belt look sportier as does apparent stitching, stitching in a different color, or layers of leather. Leather with fabric is casual as are canvas, stretch twill, ribbon/grosgrain, and thicker, wider, or more unfinished leather. Woven or braided leather belts, although less casual looking than those above, are best worn with less dressy suits or jackets/blazers.

You'll know that the belt is on the wide side if it has trouble passing easily through your belt loops. Unless you are in a part of the country where it is considered classic, avoid larger or decorated buckles with classic business casual attire. Belts that are much narrower than the classic 1 ¼" to 1 ½" width could be appropriate for business casual depending on your workplace.

It doesn't matter whether your buckle is a rectangle, often with rounded or softened ends for comfort, or an oval, but the color of the metal and how shiny or dull it appears do count.

Everyone can wear both gold/brass and silver. If you look best in clear, vibrant colors, avoid wearing dull, tarnished metals. If you look best in toned down, muted-looking colors, avoid large amounts of bright, shiny metals.

You'll look more pulled together and in-the-know if you match the metallics you are wearing. For example, your watch and belt buckle should both be either gold or silver toned. Brass buttons on a blazer should match both your watch and your belt buckle, as well as any cufflinks and shoe buckles.

Your metallic colors also need to look good together. For example, brass buttons on a blazer call for the same *shade* of gold in links, buckles, and watch—not one that appears more yellowish, pinkish, or brassy.

You can own belts with both gold-toned/brass and silver buckles, or you can buy one belt that has a buckle with both metal tones—the same goes for your watch. Another option is to wear a belt with a leather covered buckle.

YOU NEED SOLE SO DON'T
LOAFER AROUND

JUST THE BASICS

- ▲ Wear the best quality you can afford.

- ▲ With navy, black, or gray suits, wear black smooth leather lace-ups or dressy slip-ons.

- ▲ Match your belt to your shoe.

- ▲ With dressy suits and lighter weight fabrics, avoid very heavy-looking shoes, like bulky wing tips or shoes with thicker or contrasting soles.

- ▲ Penny loafers are casual slip-ons and are best worn for business casual looks and with more casual suits and jackets.

- ▲ A better quality shoe can upgrade your attire; an inexpensive shoe can downgrade it.

BEYOND THE BASICS

For classic business or classic business casual, wear a leather shoe style appropriate to the attire you are wearing that day. First to buy are generally cap-toe or plain-toe black lace-ups or, if you feel it's appropriate, dressy slip-ons with or without a tassel. The "if you feel it's appropriate" comes from the fact that my experts have different opinions when it comes to wearing slip-on shoes of any kind with a more formal business suit. Those who are more traditionally conservative in their thinking and their attire would only wear a lace-up.

If you are wearing a more casual suit or business casual attire, you can substitute penny loafers or suede lace-ups. Regardless of what you see other men doing, please do **not** wear penny loafers with a dressy suit and tie. I'm aware that this rule is broken all the time, but that doesn't mean that it is working to the wearer's advantage. The all-American look of penny loafers with gray flannels and a jacket (with or without a tie) is classic business casual.

Also, no matter what you see, hear, or read, wearing a brown shoe with a navy suit and tie renders the look business casual instead of classic business. To best tie this brown and navy look together, your necktie should have a touch of brown and navy. Along the same lines, if you ever wear a brown shoe with gray, let a tie that includes gray and brown coordinate the look—in both instances, the tie could have other colors as well.

You can turn dressy suits into business casual looks by wearing them with a nice casual shirt or sweater and a more casual shoe. Loafers are super with classic business casual attire as long as they don't look like a moccasin or have little bumps on the sole.

Generally, the smoother the leather and the plainer the shoe the dressier it will look, but that doesn't mean that you can't wear it equally as well with business casual looks. Any time a leather has more texture, like a pebble grain, it will not be as dressy as a smooth leather, but you can still wear it with a suit, just not with your dressiest attire.

A monk-strap shoe (it has buckles) is best kept for business casual unless you are wearing it to purposely give your suit an other than dressy image. Some of my experts don't like them, but if you do, please make sure that your shoe buckles match other metals you are wearing—such as your belt buckle and watch.

Wing tips that are sleek versus bulky and heavy are dressier and more flattering; a suede wing tip is more casual than its smooth leather brother, but it can still be worn with suits—just more casual suits. The classic wing tip and other heavier looking shoes look better with cuffed trousers and heavier weight fabrics—no heavy-looking wing tips with linen, for example. Shoes that combine linen or other fabrics with leather work best with lighter weight fabrics.

Canvas shoes are always sporty no matter what you paid for them. Any shoe that is cut lower than a penny loafer or higher than a classic lace-up or slip-on is generally more casual looking. With a low-cut shoe, your socks become even more important. A lace-up that is made in such a way that the leather meets (touches) across the front of the shoe, will be dressier than if you see the tongue of the shoe under the laces.

Two-toned shoes, saddle shoes, bucks, spectators, and those that are made of woven leather, or mix a variety of skins and leather, are casual.

Shoe styles with very wide square toes are not classic and can give your foot a heavy, chunky look—the most sleek-looking shoes have a more slender toe. Any shoe that has a thick sole looks heavier and more casual than the same shoe with a thinner sole.

Any shoe that is obviously not leather should be considered very, very casual. A leather lace-up or slip-on that has an obvious "other than leather" sole, like rubber, is best kept for business casual attire.

Boots—cowboy, Chelsea, hiking, or work boots—are for creative business casual but generally not for classic business casual **except** in specific geographic locations of this country. If a boot looks like it would be right at home on a motorcycle, it's not the best choice for classic business casual. The same, if it looks like it could climb a mountain. A lace-up boot, if it's not dirty, has more acceptance when worn with more casual suits (without a tie) in the western and southwestern regions of the United States.

From a quality standpoint, avoid split cowhide, most manmade materials, plastic heels, sprayed-on color, and glued soles. The best-made and most comfortable shoes will be lined in leather (comfort in all shoes should be a given).

For the best look, your shoe color should always relate to what you are wearing. Some well dressed men are wearing brown shoes with a blue suit. Many well dressed men would never do this. Keep in mind that a black shoe with a navy suit looks dressier and less fragmented—less interruption of the leg line. Even though they are hard to find, my favorite is a dark navy shoe with a navy suit (and with blue jeans, also) because I love how clean the line looks—just like it looks when you wear a black shoe with a black suit or trousers. In the shoe department, ask the sales associate if any of their styles come in navy; they will generally check the catalogs of different manufacturers.

If you choose to wear a brown shoe with navy, for the dressiest look, the shoe should be a very dark brown, and it will look best if there is a touch of brown in your tie to help tie the colors together. Try it and you'll see what I mean. It can also look more related to your coloring if you have brown hair. In a story that's been passed along for ages, the Duke of Windsor wore brown suede wing tips with a navy suit, and a friend of his remarked that it wasn't wrong to do because the Duke knew better. No matter which you choose to do most of the time, please don't wear a brown shoe with a navy suit for classic business or dressy evening or daytime occasions.

On one such evening occasion in a private club in Washington, looking around, my eyes found a very handsome man who was perfectly dressed, not only for the occasion but also for his coloring—except for his shoes. A Contrast Color Type, he was classically and stylishly dressed in a well-cut navy suit, white shirt and clear red, navy and white subtly patterned tie and dressy *brown* shoes.

Now, sometimes when I get bored, which isn't that often, a sense of mischief disrupts my normally angelic behavior and I do something that I've never done before in my life. In this case, assuming that he was visiting Washington, I wrote him a note on the back of my business card (which, of course, conveys that I am the President of Color 1 Associates, International Image and Style Consultants) the following: "Everything about the way you look is perfect except for your shoes—you must have forgotten to pack black shoes. If you need advice, please call." I handed it to him with a smile as I was leaving the club. The next day I flew off to Hawaii to conduct two days of wardrobe seminars for a corporation, forgetting all about my forward behavior. When I returned, there was the following message (in a French accent): "Hello, my name is Alain and I'm calling for advice about my shoes."

Deciding when, or whether, to wear a light, medium, or dark shoe can be a bit of a puzzle. All you really have to do to be appropriate is to always match your shoe and belt regardless of what you are wearing. If you are after more than that, work to achieve a good color balance between your shoe and your attire by using a light- or medium-tone shoe with lighter colors; a medium or dark shoe with darker colors; a light, medium, or dark shoe with medium-tone colors—all depend on the color of your shirt or jacket, the season, and even your hair color—I know, you think I'm crazy.

One of the most difficult looks to balance is all-dark on top with a light bottom, like light gray trousers with a black sweater and black blazer. Black shoes and a black belt help a lot. If the black belt has a silver buckle, all the better. If the blazer has silver buttons, fabulous. With camel/beige/cream trousers try a belt with a brass buckle and a blazer with brass buttons—essentially, you are "bringing the bottom color up."

You can make many combinations work by bringing the bottom color up, but if you **haven't** done that, *please* **don't** wear:

⊘   Light trousers with all-dark on the top with a light shoe.

⊘   Medium-toned trousers with all-dark on the top and a light shoe.

⊘   A light shoe when everything else is dark.

More and more, there is a nice range of shades of brown shoe and belt colors available. No longer is brown just brown—it's cognac and vicuna, for example. Avoid browns that are orangy or a reddish-burgundy unless you *tie* the color into your tie and/or the color is a highly visible hair color. It's also hard to find these colors in belts.

When wearing a light shoe it's best to wear a light-toned belt that matches as closely as possible—those that are leather are hard to find. Consider a light-colored buck (sort of a smoother leather version of suede) to wear with lighter colors. Suede and buck can be worn all year, but some experts feel it's best to avoid wearing suede when it is really hot outside.

What's this business about hair-colored shoes? There are two colors that are already part of every outfit you put on—your hair color and/or hair highlight color (whichever is more visible in all lighting conditions) and your skin tone. These colors are already part of your color scheme no matter what, unless you're wearing a hat that totally hides your hair. Instead of bringing in an odd color that doesn't relate to the colors you are wearing, or to you, bring in one that does. It only makes sense that if you repeat these body colors in accessories and clothing you will look really polished, sophisticated, and *pulled together*. If you have any ties that have a touch of your hair color or skin tone in them, they are probably among your favorites even though you may not have realized why.

When you need a shoe other than black, consider wearing your hair color, hair highlight color (if it is very apparent), and your skin tone, as well as lighter and darker versions of your hair color and skin tone. For those of you who want an *edge* over the competition and/or over the accepted, sometimes pedestrian-looking norm, this is an idea worth trying.

Match your hair or hair highlight color and your skin tone as closely as possible—in front of a mirror, put the shoe on the floor and glance at yourself to see if it gives the "illusion" of the color you want. Do the same if you are a redhead (some "brown" shoes will give the illusion). Although gray shoes are hard to find, if your hair is silver, or gray, it's worth the hunt.

If your hair color is light and you need a medium- or darker-colored shoe, use a camel and brown that are darker versions of your hair color (golden blonds will look for golden camels and golden browns, for example). If you need a light shoe and your hair color or skin tone is light, that's the color you are looking for. If your hair is dark and your skin tone is light, look for your skin tone. If your skin tone and hair are darker, look for a lighter version of your skin tone. If your hair color is medium in tone and you need a darker-toned shoe, use a darker version of your hair color.

If your hair is very dark brown, a black shoe will probably give the illusion you're looking for because it's a darker *version* of your hair color—your mirror will tell you if the color balance is good.

Your feet may still be growing and they may keep growing. Get measured and shop for shoes toward the end of the day when your feet will tell you what feels good. It's best to wear the type of socks that you would be wearing with the shoe.

Going without shoes would make a huge statement—as does wearing shoes that aren't well cared for. Always, always make certain that they are polished and well-heeled.

Some books recommend that you not wear the same pair of shoes two days in a row—they may be oblivious to the same budget considerations that many men have. Wooden shoe trees are the answer. To help your shoes last and look better longer, slip in shoe trees the minute you take them off. Use wood, not plastic because it will absorb any dampness and keep the toes of your shoes from curling up.

Please note that just because a shoe is made out of leather doesn't mean you can wear it to work. No sandals of any kind, not even for creative business casual. Not even for very casual business casual. Many well dressed men, even those who can afford them, feel that alligator shoes and belts are bit too showy—a little over the top. When in doubt, go for *understated elegance*.

SOCK IT TO 'EM

JUST THE BASICS

- ♟ Always wear socks.

- ♟ Experts adamantly disagree whether your socks should match your pants, your shoes, or another color in your attire, such as your shirt or tie. So, I guess that it's personal preference, but for classic business or classic business casual, when in doubt, match your socks to your shoes or your trousers.

- ♟ For creative business casual, match your socks to your wardrobe— pants, shoes, shirt or sweater, a prominent color in your tie, or even your pocket square.

- ♟ Avoid wearing lighter colored socks when both your trousers and shoes are dark unless you are doing it *on purpose* so someone will notice them.

- ♟ No socks so thin that you can see your skin through them.

- ♟ With the exception of creative business casual, avoid wearing any socks that call attention to themselves.

BEYOND THE BASICS

What's in your sock drawer? If you prefer to match your shoes and you only wear black and brown shoes, you really only need black and brown socks. If you like to match your pants and you wear navy, black, gray, brown, beige/ tan/sand, and camel, your sock drawer will have those colors.

Do you need to wear over-the-calf socks? If you ever cross your legs or sit in such a way that even a sliver of your hairy (or hair-free) leg shows, you need to always wear over-the-calf socks. Don't put yourself in the position of having to lean over to pull up your socks. If the "sock was on the other leg," you would freak if you even saw the top of a woman's knee-highs or trouser socks. It's neither appealing nor professional.

Is it really all that important? Yes. Men used to wear garters to keep their socks up and I once lost interest in a particular FBI agent because his bare legs showing above his socks projected an image of a man who was careless about his person, which infers that he might be careless in other aspects of his life.

Never have there been so many socks made in different fibers and in combinations of those, including mixes of pima cotton/nylon, cotton/wool/nylon, wool/nylon, cotton/acrylic, cotton/nylon/linen, cotton/rayon/nylon, nylon/cotton/wool/rayon, and even some with lycra. Only your feet, and how much or how little they sweat, will tell you which are best for you. Those that have the highest percentage of a natural fiber like cotton or wool will *breathe* the best, while those with a high percentage of acrylic or nylon will be the hottest.

Some socks are so thin that you can see your skin through them—this is not a good thing There are also some socks that *look too thin* for cold weather, heavy wool trousers, or heavier looking shoes. They look *out of place* and people will notice. Okay, I notice, but I'm sure I'm not the only one!

Once (no, I wasn't bored and I don't have a *thing* for socks—it just looks that way) on a stormy winter night in a wonderful steak restaurant in New York I was deeply engaged in a business discussion with my best friend, Phyllis. During our entire meal I kept feeling someone's eyes on me. Finally I glanced to my left, and there was a truly awesome looking guy (sitting with several other men) smiling at me. Yes, he was beautifully dressed, except..... He was wearing what appeared to me to be a black and brown subtle plaid jacket, a black sweater, black, warm-looking trousers with a cuff, and brown suede shoes. A really terrific color combination for him and a wonderful look for the snowy weather. The **problem**? His socks. They were *too thin* to work well with the weighty layers and the suede shoes—AND they appeared to be white.

Again, filled with a sense of mischief and perhaps wanting to find a way to return his interest, I wrote him a note on the back of my card: *Everything is perfect except for your socks—they should be a heavier weight and black or brown instead of white.* When we got up to leave, he smiled and said, "Hi." I handed him the card which he quickly tucked under his plate, probably hoping that the other guys at the table wouldn't take note.

A few days later, when I returned to Washington, he called to inform me (in a very nice way) that his socks weren't white, they were a very pale blue that matched a blue stripe in his jacket and that he had realized, when he put them on, that they were too thin for what he was wearing but he didn't want to take the time to change them—if he had, this awesome man and I might not be the super friends we still are today! In restaurant lighting, the blue stripe wasn't visible—that means that blue socks in any weight would have looked out of place even from a short distance.

Always wear socks unless the business you are in requires bare feet. Just a note about going without socks in your free time: If you are wearing a jacket, a turtleneck, or a high-necked sweater, wear socks. Being bare below doesn't make visual sense when you are completely covered up on top.

It takes both a particular personality and a categorically out of the norm work environment to pull off flamboyant socks. Solid colors, different textures, and subtle patterns are perfect for both business and business casual attire, I feel that subtle patterns can add a touch of zest and elegance to your attire, but *subtle* means that you won't want your socks to be a topic of conversation. If your socks have even a touch of cream or beige in them, it's best not to wear them with a white shirt but with a cream or beige shirt instead. Of course, your tie and suit need to be agreeable with the combination as well.

Although the good cheer that comes from wearing holiday socks during the season is generally okay except for solemn meetings, if you love adventure when it comes to your socks, it is best expressed when you are in your creative business casual mode.

LEARNING THE ABC'S OF BUSINESS CASUAL

JUST THE BASICS

- ♣ You don't have to dress down.

- ♣ When in doubt, wear a suit, a blazer, or jacket, and nice trousers with a nice shirt—with or without a tie.

- ♣ No jeans unless you are sure it's appropriate—dress them up with a jacket and a nice shirt/sweater (and tie, or not).

- ♣ No jeans **ever** that are faded, frayed, dirty looking, or ripped.

- ♣ No T-shirts unless you are sure they are acceptable—none **ever** that look like an undershirt or make you look like a tourist.

- ♣ No athletic shoes.

BEYOND THE BASICS

Learning the difference between classic business, classic business casual, typical business casual, and creative business casual can change your life. The message is loud and clear—if you are well-dressed, you will have the **edge** when it comes to promotions. I can't stress enough that I want you to look as super (read professional and appropriate) in your casual looks as you do in your suits and ties. Men wear the same thing, like khakis with a polo shirt or oxford button-down, all the time out of fear—they don't want to make a mistake.

> Fear of looking foolish or inappropriate can keep you looking humdrum and unimaginative. — JoAnna

Think casual elegance. *Yikes*, am I telling you that you need to dress up all of the time? No—it's all a matter of learning how to look pulled together, and it could involve wearing a suit or jacket but it doesn't involve wearing shorts, or short trousers, regardless of what other men you work with wear.

At some companies business casual has backfired and caused them to lose future clients and even current clients. Why? Mainly because the sloppy appearance of employees gives the impression that the company is not well run, not professional, doesn't know their stuff—they cannot be trusted to do the best job for the client. Guidelines have not been specific enough and they are not being policed well because bosses/managers are sensitive about telling their employees how to dress. Therefore some companies have moved away from a business casual policy back to formal business attire, requiring a suit and tie. Some of these firms have retained casual Fridays.

Whether you are entry level or the boss, and your company lets you dress any way you want, I hope the way you want to look is professional versus sloppy—pulled together instead of haphazard. To care about the way you look shows respect for yourself and others—wherever and whenever (even outside of work) you represent your company **and** yourself.

Regardless of the differences that exist from job to job, company to company, industry to industry, and region to region, you either look good in what you are wearing or you don't—you look *professional,* or not—leadership material, or not. Here are the ABC's and D's of strictly business and business casual:

A   **Classic Business, also known as Formal Business:** Suit, dress shirt, and tie; plain- or cap-toe lace-ups or dressy slip-ons (no penny loafers).

B   **Classic Business Casual:** Blazer or jacket, nice shirt (with or without a tie), and nice trousers; sweater may be used as a layering piece over shirt; lace-ups including suede, slip-ons including classic penny loafers.

C   **Business Casual:** Typical looks consist of nice pants including khakis and nice shirt with a collar or nice sweater; blazer or jacket not required; no denim or T-shirts; lace-ups and slip-ons can be casual, but no athletic shoes; could include non-outrageous up-fashion looks depending on industry.

D   **Creative Business Casual:** Nice pants and nice jeans; nice shirts (including nice T-shirts) and sweaters; blazer or jacket not required; lace-ups and slip-ons can be casual, but no athletic shoes; includes, but does not require, up-fashion (not flashy) looks.

NICE, **nice,** and *nice* means good-looking, quality fabrics including: merino wool in all weights, cashmere and cashmere blends, cotton in different weaves like waffle knit pique and petite pique (finer/smoother), and more silky finished cottons, mercerized cottons, linen, rayon, silk, and blends of all of these. The microfibers don't breathe so they aren't a good choice—yet. Someone is bound to develop a synthetic fiber that is cool one of these days.

One of the most important things about business casual that you should know is that you don't have to dress down. You can wear a suit and tie, or just leave your tie off. With the guidelines above, you can always go up on the list (dressier) but be careful going down (more casual). For example, business casual can always look like classic business casual or classic business—not the other way around.

If you are feeling overwhelmed or confused, just wear **A** every day because you will look appropriate no matter what, and it is not a problem if you are overdressed in comparison to your co-workers. When you want/need a **B** look, just take your tie off or wear a blazer or jacket and nice pants instead of a suit. When you have **A** and **B** down pat, and it's appropriate, you can utilize **C** and **D** looks.

Your **ABC's and D's** are more than just looks—they are a state of mind, an attitude. Also, **A, B,** and **C** can be as *creative* as **D** within their own framework. The uniqueness of each look will depend on the styling of the suit jacket and the way you combine your colors, textures, and patterns. Even the most classic business look can be stylish and/or creative.

If you don't know how to coordinate separates for business casual looks, and aren't interested in learning how, just wear a *base* with a layering piece like a jacket, sweater, or vest. An interesting layering piece would have a unique shape or pattern. To review information on the *base*, see page 105.

American casual wear is world-renowned for its style—our American designers and manufacturers do it better than anyone else. Why, then, do so many American men look unstylish in their casual clothes? Two reasons. Many have gotten too casual, partly because dress codes are not specific enough **and** they seem to think or feel that casual, grubby, and sloppy are synonyms. Secondly, men seem to be able to organize only suits and ties, and jeans and T-shirts. In between this dressy and very casual look they don't know what to do.

Even the Parisians, known worldwide for their sense of style, have become very casual, and not always in the most elegant way. Some have copied the worst of American casual—such as wearing sneakers every day.

Never fear, it's not going to happen to you because you've been training your eye and every *smart tip* you have been reading and practicing can be applied to casual attire. All of the principles are the same, only the styling, fabrics, and detailing may be more casual.

⊘ **Bad Advice:** Wear your tennis shoes with a wool crepe suit in the summer.

① **My Advice:** Not unless you want to be noticed for the wrong reason.

> Good taste is not an old-fashioned concept. — JoAnna

What makes a great shirt or sweater for a business casual look? It will have a little extra something. Unusually elegant fabric, distinctive texture, interesting pattern, unique stitching—a personality. Light-weight silk shirts look too diaphanous, too flimsy, and too thin for business casual.

Can you wear nice jeans? It depends. If I am using the word "jeans," as in recommending them with a specific look, I am assuming that your particular business casual allows them at least on certain days. If they don't, then just wear these looks in your free time.

Do I think that jeans should be allowed for business casual? Yes, **BUT** only if your **total** look is excellent and appropriate—equal to all of your other great looks, just *different* from them. And I really would love for you to wear a jacket with them—it will set you apart. No? Your choice. Will you at least wear one to and from work? No? I give up—I'm out of the business. Well, just a few more pages of *suggestions*. No fading, no fraying, no rips, no holes, no exceptions.

If T-shirts are permitted, look for those of quality fabric that have a more tapered sleeve versus a square, wide, boxy sleeve—the look is more refined and will fit better under your jackets. Unless you work in an environment where they will serve your career goals, avoid tight muscleman T-shirts with short, tight sleeves that end in the middle of your biceps.

A suit with a more casual shirt? Definitely do double-duty with your suits by wearing them with nice T-shirts (if allowed), turtlenecks, crewnecks, high V-necks, polo shirts and nice looking odd shirts sometimes referred to as sport shirts. Think of a business casual T-shirt as a high neck pullover made out of a very nice fabric. If anyone could ever mistake it for a typical T, it's not to be worn for typical business casual.

A nice plaid or print shirt turns a suit into a business casual look, but if you wear a shirt like this out, as a "jacket," or layered over another shirt or sweater it becomes an extremely casual look.

Can you wear a pin-striped or chalk-striped suit for business casual without a tie? Since I would love the look, I would love to give you a blanket "Yes." So, "Yes," **but**—there goes the blanket—think twice before wearing it for classic business casual because casual and striped suit are generally not found in the same thought and may be a bit up-fashion for some classic business casual atmospheres.

- ⊘ **Bad Advice?** Almost any sport jacket will work with khakis or jeans.

- ⏏ **My Advice:** Yes, ONLY IF the color of your jeans or khakis is apparent in the jacket.

For the most coordinated look, your shirt or sweater will match the stripe or the background color. The same advice goes if you are wearing a plaid, tweed, check, or herringbone suit without a tie. With these suits, I think you would look totally appropriate even for classic business casual. When you aren't wearing a tie, it is sometimes possible to use a pocket square to bring together an otherwise less color-coordinated look. For example, wear a gray and white striped suit with a blue shirt and blue pocket square—to make this look work well, you must keep your jacket on. Change to a gray or white shirt and you will still look pulled together without the jacket.

Utilizing your trousers and vest from your 3-piece suit gives a 2-color dressy business casual look—wear them with, or without, an odd jacket.

First, for those of you who refuse to be deterred by wrinkles, try linen suits in the summer. Second, try linen in a stripe. Third, borrow the jacket from either to wear over a base or with other separates, keeping in mind that you now know how to successfully tie the colors together. Wear a super quality T-shirt under your linen pin-stripe—it can match either color in the stripe, or, as in the example above, add a pocket square in the color of your shirt.

When wearing a tie with a casual shirt style or casual shirt fabric, make sure that the tie isn't a silky/satiny/shiny fabric (that only works well with very dressy-looking dress shirts).

An all-white or soft white, cream, beige/tan/sand *base* of matching trousers and shirt or sweater is an excellent warm-weather look for business casual unless you feel you need to stay in darker neutrals for your industry. Consider a winter white/cream wool *base* when it's cold outside. Match your belt and shoes and layer with a terrific jacket in any solid color (Gentle and Muted Color Types will avoid the navy or black with white). Jackets in plaids or checks should have at least a touch of the color of the *base*.

Synonyms for casual include: careless, haphazard, hasty, indifferent, and indiscriminate. None of these things are what any company has in mind when they tell their employees that they can "dress down." — JoAnna

---

Because of the popularity of business casual, your blazer and sport coat wardrobe has become even more important. If you find that you rarely wear a suit (because no one working around you does) collect odd jackets to express your personal style. Just make sure that you are wearing these jackets with shirts and trousers that are coordinated from a color standpoint—for the most pulled together look, the color of both should be highly visible in the jacket.

Jackets with a throat tab (they button up around your neck) are casual—personally, I love them, but the only time you can wear them buttoned at the neck is when you're outside in the cold.

Classic polo shirts can have a good business casual look when they are made out of a quality fabric and they are *newer*. Once they have been washed just one time too many, they need to be relegated to washing the car. Their life will be longer if they are not put in the dryer. No big baggy sleeves that hang to your elbow, please.

Cotton knit polo style shirts with khakis are the business casual, no-brainer uniform for many men. If you always want to look a cut above, wear polo shirts in a luxurious fabric with a jacket and nice wool pants or a suit instead of always with khakis lest you run the risk of looking like every other man. A good rule of thumb is when you try something on and you *feel* casual or sporty in it, do not wear it for any business attire unless sporty/casual is the feel/look you are striving for.

Just because you dress down an otherwise dressy suit with a sweater or polo shirt doesn't mean you can wear dockers or athletic shoes—wear the same lace-up or slip-on shoes you would wear when you have on a shirt and tie or choose a slightly more casual shoe like a penny loafer.

> Wearing a jacket instantly makes casual attire more important—always wearing one could become your *signature statement.* — JoAnna

What about wearing a leather jacket? Classic James Dean, only for creative business casual. Change the style, deleting the zippers, and you get a *maybe*. A leather jacket in a sport coat style, versus a motorcycle jacket style, has a place in some casual businesses, but not in others. A leather jacket with matching buttons is dressier looking than one with a zipper, and a leather jacket with a matching zipper is dressier looking than one with a gold-toned or silver-toned zipper.

How about a jeans jacket? If denim is worn freely at your place of business, then a denim jacket might be appropriate. A typical jeans jacket is very, very casual (add several more very's if it is faded or distressed). Can it be worn with a shirt and *casual* tie? If the other men you work with, including those at the highest levels, wear jeans and T-shirts, you could look good and interesting. Adding a layering piece like a jacket, sweater, vest, or tie gives denim or casual pants some style. Although casual, a jeans jacket worn over a *base* (pants or jeans and shirt or sweater are the same color) is dressier looking than the same jacket with pants or jeans and a top that don't match.

Dark blue denim and black denim are much dressier looking than medium and light blue and very much dressier looking than faded and/or distressed or already dirty looks. Also remember that denim comes in gray—which I happen to love on men with silver in their hair because it looks so pulled together.

Can you/should you wear striped T-shirts? Not for classic business casual. Yes, a nice one for other business casual (I'm not talking about rugby shirts). I love the look of a quality striped T-shirt with a solid-color suit—just make sure that one of the colors in the shirt is the color of the suit. When worn with an odd jacket and pants, both colors should be in the shirt. Note that there is a difference between a classic polo shirt and the extremely casual rugby shirt known for its wide, often colorful stripes.

Except perhaps for creative business casual, please don't wear your shirt out when you are wearing a jacket—there's a difference, sometimes big, sometimes small, between looking sloppy and dressing in a creative casual way.

Even if your casual dress code allows it, I don't recommend athletic shoes (sneakers) or deck shoes/topsiders for business casual attire. No, not even if they are new. Not even if they cost more that your dressy cap-toe lace-ups.

When it comes to your wardrobe, doubt means "No." Why? Because leaving the house unsure of how you look can affect your entire day, the way you interact with co-workers and clients, even with someone on the phone, including your significant other. Only you know your place of business, its spoken and unspoken standards, and your career goals. When in doubt, save it for the weekend.

What's the best business casual look? Among the best are a suit with an interesting shirt or sweater and nice trousers with an interesting shirt or sweater and an odd jacket. *Easy elegance* isn't hard and it's never a look that says "you tried too hard."

PULLING IT ALL TOGETHER

JUST THE BASICS

- ♠ The *easy, elegant* way to combine odd jackets, shirts, and trousers into perfectly pulled together business casual looks is to wear a tie that has at least a touch of those colors.

- ♠ If you don't want to wear a tie, make sure that your separates balance each other by combining colors that have a relationship with each other, like wearing light, medium, and dark values of the same color.

- ♠ Color balance is also achieved by wearing different colors that are closer together in value like a light color with another light color, light with medium, medium with medium, or medium with dark.

- ♠ Einstein gave up and had identical suits made.

BEYOND THE BASICS

Knowing that you look great can build confidence in other areas of your life. Many men are confident wearing a suit and tie and they are self-assured when it comes to wearing their jeans—for looks in between, they are at a loss. Learning how to combine separates to create super looks is fun, and not really that difficult—like learning a new trick on your computer that will make your life easier forever (for me, it was learning how to use find and replace).

The secret is in the color coordination of the jacket or blazer with the trousers, shirt or sweater, and tie (if you are wearing one). The colors of your belt and shoes also come into play. Wearing your best colors and color combinations, as well as the way your clothes fit you, are important givens.

A quick review of your best color combinations on page 67 would be helpful. The overall most flattering looks for each Color Type are:

 Gentle coloring—blended.

 Muted coloring—blended but gutsy.

 Contrast coloring—precise, crisp contrast and bold.

 Light-Bright coloring—precise, crisp contrast but not bold.

If you haven't yet figured out your Color Type go to page 46. Keeping that in mind as you read the following will help you create looks that are more specifically **super** on **you**.

The formula for combining odd jackets, trousers, shirts, and ties that works every time seems to be a *secret* since so few men utilize it. Using it guarantees that you will look pulled together, sophisticated, polished, and appropriate. Utilizing your separates (or the pieces of your suits as separates) in this way literally doubles your wardrobe without spending much, if any, money, and it will increase the individuality of your look—an excellent start on building a professional and *smart wardrobe.*

The Secret of the *Perfect* Tie

The secret is to make sure that your tie has at least a touch of the colors of your shirt, trousers, and jacket, or that, on their own, without a tie, you look *smart* because the colors of each garment balance each other.

For example, if you wear gray flannels off and on all fall and winter with blue shirts and a navy blazer, you will want to wear them with ties that combine gray, blue, and navy. If you also wear your gray trousers with a white shirt and a black jacket, you will want to wear them with a tie that combines gray, white, and black—these ties could incorporate other colors if you like.

Whenever you buy trousers, jackets (or suits), and shirts in new colors, start looking for ties in combinations that will pull your new pieces together, allowing you the *easy elegance* of combining some of your old favorites with your new.

You might find pulling your looks together easier if you:

◆ First decide which suit, or jacket and trousers, you want to wear.

◆ Select a tie that has the color of the suit in it or both jacket and trouser colors in it.

◆ Last, pick a shirt in a color, or neutral that is also in the tie and then check the total look, adjusting the shirt color if necessary.

If you have a tie you love but aren't wearing, check it with all of your suits and odd jackets to see if you can make a good marriage—then wear it with a shirt that perfects the ensemble.

You can't always trust the color combinations you see on display in the stores, men's magazines, or catalogs—not even a manufacturer's idea of what looks good. Sometimes they do a good job, sometimes not so great, because they aren't specialists in color.

Many years ago, before I was given the highest award in the image consulting industry for being one of the founders, my first husband (I've only had one but I lovingly refer to him as my first) used to trust my advice. We shopped together for his clothes (sometimes I shopped for him) and I coordinated everything and laid his suit, shirt, and tie out for him each morning—because he wanted me to.

The looks we created for him were very presidential in his strictly business attire and creative business casual for less serious business. When he would walk down a hallway, people (mostly women) used to come flying out of offices to talk with him—their excuse was that they wanted to know where he bought what he was wearing. One day, when I was out of town, he bought a suit without me and he was so pleased that it had an extra pair of trousers that made the suit into a sport coat look. So was I until I saw the color of the extra pair of pants—they didn't go with the suit jacket. When I told him he said, "Surely the manufacturer knows more than you." No, that's not why we aren't married any longer, but it took me a while after he apologized (someone else whose taste he respected also told him they didn't look good together) before I started laying out his clothes again.

Is a white or soft white shirt always appropriate? From a business standpoint, yes. BUT it doesn't always work from a color-coordinated, pulled together look with every tie and/or every suit or jacket. If you love white shirts and truly want the easiest elegance of never wearing (or having to buy) a shirt of another color, don't purchase a suit, jacket, or tie that won't work with a white shirt. Review the best whites for you on page 90.

With some exceptions, of course, whenever you wear a white shirt or a shirt with a white collar, make sure that your tie includes a touch of white—the **same** white—pure white shirt with pure white in the tie, soft white with soft white, cream with cream. Many ties have a touch of silvery white that generally works with pure white and soft white shirts, as well as light gray shirts, suits and trousers.

You want the *easy elegance* but would like a bit of variety with your shirts? It's easy and elegant to be obvious. For example, wear a gray and white striped shirt with a dark gray jacket, medium gray trousers, and a gray and white tie.

A blue and white striped shirt, navy jacket, and light gray trousers would look polished with a navy, light silver (that gives a white look), and gray tie. You can add other colors to these combinations as long as you keep the color of the jacket, trousers (or suit), and at least one of the shirt colors in the tie.

Let me say the second part of that again, *keep at least one of the shirt colors in the tie.* A red and white striped shirt worn with black trousers and a black suit or jacket will work with a black and white tie. Why? The tie includes two of the three colors. Also, every outfit has a much better chance of looking terrific without a jacket when the tie contains the color of your trousers. Make sure that your look will stand alone without a jacket, because the minute you remove it you are bound to have an encounter where you wish you had it on.

- $\oslash$ **Bad Advice:** Wear a black suit with a red and white striped shirt and a maroon and gold tie and brown shoes.

- $\oplus$ **My Advice:** No color harmony exists in this combination because neither of the colors in the tie relate to the shirt or suit. And please don't wear brown shoes with a black suit unless your tie "ties" in the brown. Very few people know how to combine colors well, let alone in a flattering way for their coloring. If you master this art, you will have an unbeatable edge.

Please don't wear a striped shirt of any kind with a tweed, herringbone, plaid, or other pattern jacket or suit UNLESS the colors in the shirt are very visible in the pattern and you promise me that it is equal to or better than your best look.

Although most looks are best kept to two patterns at the most, the very adventuresome can wear a striped or checked shirt and a patterned tie with an other than solid suit or jacket IF they all have the identical colors and the same overall look. Blended with blended. Contrast with contrast. When tempted to put this look together, again ask yourself the "equal to or better than" question. When wearing other than solid suits and jackets, it's generally best to keep your shirt a solid color, one that is apparent in the suit and jacket, and then add a patterned tie that includes those colors.

Having trouble finding the perfect tie or still uncertain? You will always look elegant in a solid-color tie that matches one of the colors in your jacket, but if your pants are a different color, the tie needs to include a touch of that color as well.

Keep on the lookout for ties that combine the colors you wear most often—your **core** colors. If you love white shirts and navy, black, and gray suits, blazers, jackets, and trousers, collect ties that include at least a touch of white (or light silvery white) to tie in your shirt, and at least one or two of these **core** colors.

One of my clients, an international lawyer, can travel the world for both business and pleasure with very few pieces of clothing because everything works with almost everything else.

For example, a tie that has light silvery white, gray, black, and red will look good with both gray and black suits/blazers/jackets. One that has navy, blue, gray, and a touch of white coordinates very well with both your navy and gray suits/blazers/jackets (and you can probably successfully substitute a blue shirt, or a blue and white striped shirt, for the white if the blue in your tie is from the same color family as your shirt—perfect looks for travel mix-and-match.

You can also get some good combinations by wearing a tie that includes a darker version of your shirt color (like a dark gray, silver, and navy tie with a light gray shirt and either a gray or navy suit or jacket and trousers—again, *please* keep your best color combinations in mind.

The *Formula* for Creating Color Balance and Coordination Without a Tie

Can you look pulled together without having to wear a tie? Yes, there are several ways, the easiest of which is to wear a *base* because when your shirt and trousers match, the bottom color is already "up." For example, without a tie that includes gray, a navy and white striped shirt worn with a navy blazer and gray trousers doesn't work as well even though it has two of the three colors in it, because there is nothing to tie in the color of the trousers. You will always look more coordinated when you bring a touch of the bottom color "up."

What about using a jacket, vest, or sweater to bring the bottom color up? Absolutely, but it only counts **if** you are certain that you'll leave it on. A jacket that combines the colors of your trousers and shirt or sweater is a good look—for example, a blue and gray tweed jacket with gray flannels and a blue shirt—wear the same jacket over your blue jeans base.

Often just wearing matching shoes and belt can pull a look together— your belt brings the bottom color "up." Sometimes your hair color can give you needed balance. If your hair is very dark brown or black and you are wearing black or brown trousers with a shirt or sweater in any other color, your hair color can give the illusion of bringing the bottom color "up," making you appear coordinated. If your hair color is blond, or light brown, and you are wearing beige, camel, or light brown trousers, you can get the same effect. Silver hair elegantly ties in the colors of gray and sand/stone.

Wearing colors that have similar values (two light colors together, for example) can create a well coordinated, balanced appearance. Keeping your best color combinations in mind, here are some examples for you to try:

 A light color with another light color, like light gray trousers with a light blue shirt or sweater—if your coloring is strong, you may need to add a medium or dark layer to strengthen this color combination—a layer can be a sweater, vest, or jacket.

 White or soft white, cream, and beige work well with pastels— Contrast and dark-haired Muted Color Types may need to strengthen this combination.

 White and soft white can balance brights.

 A medium color with another medium color, such as camel trousers with a medium gray shirt or sweater.

 A dark color with another dark color, like navy and charcoal—if your coloring is subtle-looking, you will need to lighten up these darker color combinations by layering with lighter colors, or just avoid them. If your coloring needs more contrast to look your best, add a bright or light layer.

 High-contrast, like a navy or black with white or soft white, can look balanced with bright colors.

 Bright colors and medium-value slightly toned down and toned down colors will balance black, navy, and dark brown—combinations that some Color Types should avoid unless they add a layer that will lighten the look. See page 67 to review your best color combinations.

 Blended weaves of muted fabrics can balance quiet, muted colors.

Keep Mixing It Up

Since I'm an advocate of pulling your suits apart and wearing each piece as an odd jacket or odd trousers, can you ever wear a pin-striped jacket with solid-color matching trousers? More of a creative casual look, it is not recommended for strictly business firms or important meetings when the other participants don't know you. But otherwise, why not? You've read it before, the pieces of your suits are not glued together.

All you need is a strong sense of self and a touch of courage to be different. To keep this look pulled together, wear trousers in the color that matches the background color in your jacket—dark blue pin-striped jacket, with dark blue trousers, for example. Could you wear the same dark blue pin-striped jacket with dark blue jeans, white pants, or white jeans? I say it depends on where you're going and what you want to accomplish when you get there. Where do you work? Doubt means no, at least for the moment. I love it when men dress in creative elegant looks, but then I'm not your boss.

Could you wear the pin-striped, chalk-striped or plaid/check/ tweed/herringbone trousers from a suit with a sweater or just a special shirt? I say, "Of course," but what do my experts say? I asked them from a personal standpoint—would *they* do it? One said, "No, but that's not to say that it's wrong." Another said, "No, but it could look great." Others (younger men) said "Yes." The oldest expert said "No!" The only shirt and sweater colors that will work well are those that match one of the prominent colors in the pants.

All Color Types can mix black and medium or light blue (like a black suit with a blue shirt), but, although it's not impossible, it's generally not flattering to mix black and navy or black and dark blue. For example, avoid wearing a black sweater with a navy suit. If you really want to wear this combination anyway, layer a patterned shirt under the sweater that combines the black and navy with another light color or switch the sweater for a shirt and wear a tie that repeats the colors.

When you are putting odd separates together, and you're combining two values of the same color, like light gray trousers with a darker gray jacket, remember that it is important that the colors—in this example, gray—are from the same color family. A camel jacket that has a golden tone to it will combine well with golden brown trousers but not with chocolate brown trousers.

Should you avoid wearing light-colored suits in the winter? This is a part "regional," part traditional answer. Generally and traditionally speaking, if you live in a climate where it doesn't get very cold, like Florida and Southern California, you can wear any color suit year round. If you live in a strictly four-season climate, keeping your light suits for spring, summer, and September days that are hot is "expected," although definitely not required. For important meetings and occasions, it is best to wear expected attire. If you don't agree with the tradition, you may want to go with the flow until you check out what other men in your line of work are doing, or until you get to the point in your career that you can go against the grain.

Don't be afraid to wear a light-colored jacket over a fall/winter looking *base* of flannel trousers and matching merino wool sweater. The color of the base could be any of your neutrals like gray, navy, brown, or black. This super look works best for business casual as well as after-work activities (like non-formal/non-dark blue suit holiday get-togethers and dates). Do the same in the summer, just with lighter weight fabrics.

Can you wear an all one-color look for business? By all one-color I'm referring to all black or all gray, for example—gray suit, gray shirt, and gray tie. If you are in a creative field and you know it's appropriate, then of course. BUT, if you are going to be meeting with a client who is more conservative or traditional, I'd advise against it because of the trust factor—see page 24.

A good way to achieve a similar look, but one that can be worn without reproach, is to wear all of the same color, just in lighter and darker values. All blues, for example, in a light to dark range—navy suit, light blue dress shirt, and medium blue tie. To assure that the colors work well together, **they need to all be from the same color family**.

For those of you who don't want to be bothered with any of this mixing and matching of separates, the solution is easy and elegant—always wear a **base** or a **suit**. In both instances, you will look very well coordinated because the bottom color has already been tied into the top.

ACE THE INTERVIEW

JUST THE BASICS

- ♠ Look credible.

- ♠ Solid-color navy or gray suit.

- ♠ 2- or 3-button style—2-button, center vent for very conservative firms.

- ♠ White or soft white shirt, impeccably pressed.

- ♠ Wear a tie that has touches of your suit and shirt colors.

- ♠ Black shoes (not brown), navy or black socks (gray or black if you are wearing a gray suit), and a black belt.

- ♠ Safest jewelry—none or single ring on ring finger (next to little finger).

- ♠ Cover any body art if possible.

- ♠ No gum, obviously no smoking, no noisy coins in your pocket.

- ♠ Employers do not expect recent grads to be expensively dressed, but they do expect them to be neat and clean.

- ♠ Remember to smile and maintain good eye contact.

BEYOND THE BASICS

You are going to be sized up in a hurry—in just seven seconds the interviewer will make a judgment about you—do you look right for the job? When qualifications, skills, and credentials are close, the way you look will give you the edge. What you don't need is someone looking at you *wondering* if

Business Casual

A suit paired with a sweater or a shirt is the answer to easy elegance for business casual.

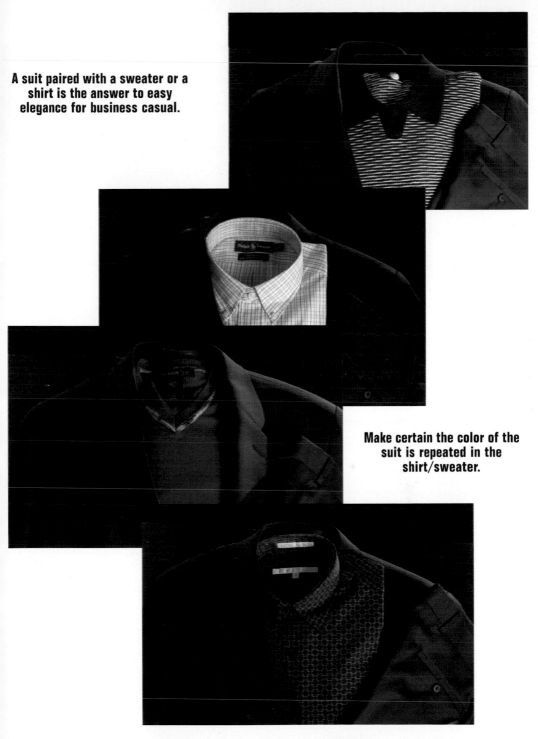

Make certain the color of the suit is repeated in the shirt/sweater.

Clothing and accessories courtesy of Macy's.
Photos courtesy of The Photographer's Gallery.

To add variety to your suits and mixed suit looks, collect shirts and ties in unusual (those you would not normally choose), yet elegant, color combinations .

Remember that the "secret" to looking pulled together (like you know what you are doing) is to make sure that your tie contains the colors of your jacket, trousers, and shirt.

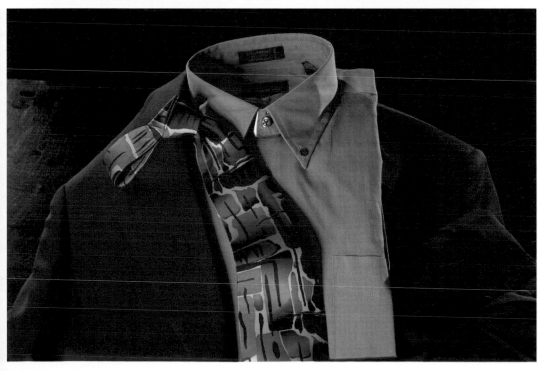

The Base: Wearing matching trousers and a sweater/shirt is an easy, elegant way to add versatility to your wardrobe – change your jacket, change your look.

When your jacket, trousers, and shirt are three different colors, it's always a more casual look. The right tie combines the three colors and creates a "pulled together" look.

you can do the job. A huge majority of firms, regardless of the their dress codes, expect you to wear a suit for an interview.

What is "fail-safe" interview attire? Fail-safe I can't promise, but if you are dressed in what is expected attire for interviews you will have your second best visual shot at making a good impression. Second best? If you are also wearing colors and a color combination that are flattering to your coloring, you will have a visual edge over everyone else who hasn't learned this skill.

It used to be that different industries had completely different expected dress codes and it wasn't necessary to put it in writing because everyone understood—wearing casual clothing wasn't an option. Now, a firm in a conservative industry, such as accounting, law, or banking, might have a 24/7 business casual **agreement** with their employees with the understanding that they need to wear a suit and tie if they are going to be meeting with a client. Many companies in creative industries, like advertising, public relations, the arts, and the high tech fields, have been less buttoned up for years. With sales and marketing firms, dress codes have often depended on the product you are selling and your target audience.

Today is a whole new ball game. Whether specifically stated or not, the appropriate attire will depend on the company, your position in that company and what you do there as well as the position you want, where you live (the region and/or city), and, perhaps, who you will be meeting with on any given day. *Always be prepared for one of the most important days of your life.*

Before an interview, if you have the opportunity to check it out, stop by the company where you will be interviewing ahead of time (in the morning or over lunch) and "people watch" to get an idea of the way the employees dress. Regardless of what you see, you will almost always still want to wear a suit, white or soft white shirt, and tie to your interview. You can also call the human resources office and ask about the dress code or the *expected* attire for an interview. **But** even if you are told casual, **please** still strongly consider wearing a suit and tie.

I used the word "almost" above. What's appropriate, and what will make an excellent impression for an interview, will depend on your industry, what job you are interviewing for, and what city you are in. If you know that even the CEO of this company wears jeans to work, maybe you can wear a navy blazer with gray trousers (khakis are more casual yet), a white shirt, and tie. I understand that even this blazer look may seem really dressed up for you, but if you want the job, your instant impression needs to be great. Use clothing as a tool—think of it as a necessary skill that is needed to get the job you want.

Is it okay to wear a double-breasted suit? There are differing opinions among the experts on whether or not you should wear a double-breasted style suit for an interview. What do I think? When in doubt wear single-breasted. If you choose to wear a double-breasted, make sure you can unbutton and button your jacket with ease, like you've been doing it for years, because you will want to arrive/meet with it buttoned, unbutton it while you are seated, and button it again when you stand up. All my experts agree that you should avoid wearing anything other than a solid-color suit—in other words, no checks, plaids, or stripes.

Try not to have a lot of stuff to gather up from the reception room (umbrella, briefcase, coat) because when someone calls your name it can feel awkward getting it all together, as it will be again when your interview is finished. Keep organized.

What do you wear when you go back for your second interview? Since you will more than likely have a second and perhaps even a third interview, what you wear when you make your next impression is as important as the first. Why? Because you won't want to *disappoint*—you don't want to cast any doubt that their first impression of you might have been wrong. You have set a standard that you will want to maintain.

If you have a second suit, let's say you wore solid navy for the first interview, you will wear your solid gray for your second. For the third, you will wear the navy again. If you only have one suit, wear it to all interviews with a change of ties. For a less conservative company you could vary your look by using a shirt other than white or soft white, such as blue (just remember that it isn't as dressy and if this is the day you are going to meet the big boss, or might even run into her/him, wear a white or soft white shirt.

What if you don't own a suit? If wearing a suit to an interview is not possible for you at this time, wear a navy blazer or gray, or even black, jacket with gray trousers, a white or soft white shirt, and a tie that combines your colors. If gray trousers aren't possible right now, wear clean, well pressed khakis. If you can't wear a jacket at this time, wear a white shirt and tie with the nicest pants you own. Remember that if you have the time to look around the discount/off-price stores you can find some very good suits, jackets, trousers, shirts, ties, socks, and shoes for a minimal amount of money.

Think twice before wearing a suit in olive, tan/khaki/beige, sand, white, or cream to a conservative meeting or an interview. Ask yourself: Who am I going to the meeting with? Who's going to be there and how will they be dressed? How do I want to be perceived? Will their perception of me match the impression I want to leave?

Walking into an interview or a meeting, you really are sized up instantly—usually not in a "let me check this person out" way, but instinctively our eyes take it all in, our brains process our impressions, and we are predisposed to judge. Let the outside match the inside—make sure you look like you have the skills that you have. Remember to smile. No, you don't have to grin all the time, just smile once in a while.

What do you wear to work on your first day of a new job besides a smile? If your job calls for a suit, wear the same one you wore to your first interview—you could select a different shirt and tie. If your workplace is business casual, plan to dress better than the men you will be working with, and keep reading.

ATTACHMENTS

JUST THE BASICS

- ♣ No sporty looking watches with business or classic business casual attire.

- ♣ Match metals of blazer buttons, belt buckle, and cufflinks.

- ♣ No large, opulent, or glitzy cufflinks.

- ♣ Buy braces, not suspenders.

- ♣ No bulging wallets—or pockets.

- ♣ No inexpensive looking pens.

- ♣ Best to avoid earrings, bracelets, and more than one ring for interviews.

- ♣ No casual canvas backpacks with classic business or classic business casual attire.

BEYOND THE BASICS
Your Watch

Some men have been inspired to start collecting watches because they realize that generally one watch just doesn't work well with everything, and besides, it's fun. You don't have to collect watches, but you do need to consider them in the overall look you want to project. Here are some of the most common mistakes that you will want to avoid:

- ⊘ Wearing a watch that doesn't make the same statement as your attire, like a sport watch with a suit or classic blazer, for example.

- ⊘ Wearing a watch that has a band in a color that doesn't go with your attire or look good with your skin tone.

- ⊘ Wearing a watch that is silver in tone when your blazer buttons are brass or vice versa—collect one that combines both gold and silver so it will work with all buckles, buttons, and cufflinks regardless of their color.

- ⊘ Wearing a watch that has a face that is too white for your skin tone—it will look inexpensive on you if you are a Gentle or Muted Color Type. The white will be the first thing your eye goes to when you glance at it, especially if the numbers are black. An off-white or cream face will be *so* much richer looking.

All that *glitters* doesn't make you look rich. If you are wearing a gold watch or cufflinks, make sure that they are a subtle tone, because bright shiny gold can look flashy, especially on Gentle and Muted Color Types.

If you love watches and want to collect them, they could become your *signature statement.* Include vintage styles and your dad's and grandfather's watches.

Sporty funky/fun watches are best worn with very casual attire only or creative business casual. For classic business, classic business casual, and dressy evening, always err on the side of subtle elegance.

If you don't look good in black, avoid watch faces and watchbands that are black. If you are a Contrast or Light-Bright Color Type, you may want to avoid a brushed silver or toned down stainless band because it can tend to look gray against your skin. If you are wearing this watch only with gray, no problem.

Do your ring and watch have to match? It's much better if they do—yet another reason to own a watch that combines both gold and silver tones, especially if you wear a gold wedding band on the same hand. Yes, I know that some stylish men say not to bother with this detail—try it both ways and judge for yourself.

A men's wardrobing book, not mine, said that watches with black leather bands are out of style. They are **always in style**—they are classic, classy, and elegant. Leather bands with contrasting stitching and/or thick or more casual looking leather are best kept for business casual and casual attire.

Braces

It has been said that men wear braces and boys wear clip-on suspenders. Friends and my experts who wear them swear by them for comfort and ease—they keep your trousers at the perfect level allowing them to fit loosely enough to be very comfortable and adapting to *temporary* weight gain. They make an interesting statement, and wearing them every day could become your *signature.* You could collect new as well as vintage braces just as another man would collect watches.

Their downside? The colors and patterns of your braces need to be coordinated with your shirts, ties, suits, jackets, and trousers. You can look at this as an opportunity to hone your skill at combining patterns and colors, or you can just wear solid colors. Your tailor or any laundry/dry-cleaning establishment will know how to properly position the buttons for your braces on the inside of your trouser waistband.

The adjustable metal piece on braces need to match your belt buckle, watch, etc. For the most coordinated appearance, the leather needs to match your shoes or a color in your tie or suit.

Cuff Links

Those that sparkle are for dressy evening only, and those that are larger than average are not fitting for classic attire. Antique links are wonderful and could be a *signature* for you.

Your Pen

Please, no cheap looking pens with advertising from other companies, banks, or free giveaways. A handsome, stylish pen makes a nice impression and you don't have to pay a king's ransom for one. Handsome simply means good-looking, not opulent, and a stylish pen is one that shows some personality. You can actually buy one at one of the big office supply stores for under $15—you'll want to keep track of it because, just like socks and gloves, pens tend to disappear.

Briefcase, Laptop Bag, Backpack

Backpacks are more casual looking than a briefcase or laptop bag, but a nice looking one (leather, not canvas) could be carried with casual suits and business casual looks. If you buy quality, you can carry a briefcase or laptop bag "forever." When a quality leather bag gets beat-up looking, it still looks good—it is thought of as having *character*. If the quality wasn't so good to begin with, it just looks like you need to replace it. The most expensive are lined in the same leather as the outside. Bags made of reptile are considered ostentatious by many men. Best colors include the color of the shoes you wear most often, your most used neutrals, and your hair color.

Pocket Squares

Solid-color pocket squares are *easy elegance*—just match one of the colors in your tie, shirt, or jacket. Patterns are wonderful, though tricky, because they need to coordinate with any other pattern(s). There is a rule of order among men that your tie and pocket square shouldn't match exactly. I know that this practice sounds impractical, especially when you are trying so hard to look pulled together, but it has to do with looking too "arranged," too professionally decorated, too precise—like you are trying too hard.

Please don't use a pocket square in a toned down color or blended looking pattern with a suit, jacket, shirt, or tie that has more contrast or boldness. The same goes for using a bright or boldly patterned pocket square with blended or muted-looking suits, jackets, shirts, and ties. Neither shows the other off to good advantage—they fight with each other instead of complimenting each other, and you end up looking like you don't have a clue. Also, a very important reminder, clear colors or muted colors, but not both, are flattering to you.

Avoid using a white pocket square or handkerchief with a tie that has cream or beige instead of white. Also, wearing a pure white square with a blended looking suit, shirt, or tie, like a classic glen plaid suit, for example, will make the softer white in the suit appear to be dirty.

A pocket square, generally made of silk, a very fine cotton, or linen, is for a decorative purpose only—a handkerchief is something you blow your nose on. If you are using a cotton or linen handkerchief in your breast pocket, for emergencies you may, of course, use it to dry happy or sad tears, or for your nose. After use, it is then placed in a different pocket.

Cotton and linen handkerchiefs that are used in the breast pocket need to be well ironed, but that doesn't mean that you have to press and/or starch the little pointed ends all into a row. When the edges are beautifully finished, they look nice just gathered up in your hand and tucked in your pocket with the points sticking out.

There are many appropriate ways to place a pocket square in your breast pocket, and the most careless, carefree way is generally the most elegant as long as not too much of the fabric is showing—it shouldn't look as though it's going to fall out. Avoid too much perfection/precision, as you could end up looking *stuffy*. An *easy, elegant* way to arrange a silk square is to just gather it up in the middle with the pointed ends facing down and put it in your pocket, pointed ends in first, or pointed ends up.

Rings

There is a difference of opinion on how many rings an elegant man would wear. My advice is that for classic business and classic business casual, wear one ring only. Definitely consider this advice for interviews. Some experts feel that a man can get away with one ring on each hand—like a wedding band on one and a college ring on the other. Other experts advise against wearing a college ring, period; they are usually the same men who would advise against a monogram on the cuff of your sleeve. It comes down to personal opinion and what kind of a statement you want to make.

Other Jewelry

Unfortunately, even in the new millennium, not everyone is open-minded when it comes to necklaces, earrings, and bracelets on men—especially in a classic business or classic business casual atmosphere. You get to decide if wearing them is worth the risk of not realizing your personal goals. My advice is that when in doubt, do not wear them to an interview or a conservative place of business until you get a feel for the environment.

FOCUS ON SUCCESS ᏮᏉ

JUST THE BASICS

ᏮᏉ Glasses are a major part of looking great and they need to look as excellent on you as your clothing.

ᏮᏉ There are many important basics—please scan the list below.

Beyond the Basics

I want your glasses to be perfect for you and this is one of the times I wish I could see you in person. What should you look for when you are trying on new glasses or evaluating those you are wearing now?

Here are some *smart tips* that will help you take control of how you look in glasses:

- Many of the smaller glasses are good-looking, some are interesting looking, and others look *far-out*, but you need to make sure that **you** look good and interesting—not just your glasses.

- Do they make your eyes appear closer together? It's not a good look.

- Do they make your nose appear bigger?

- Are they so close to your face that they tend to rest on your face? Smile and see if they touch your cheeks?

- Do they sit too far forward so there is too much space between the lenses and your face?

- Are they too wide for your face—coming out on the sides so far out that you can see your temples through the lenses?

- Are they too narrow for your face, making your eyes look closer together or making your face appear out of balance?

- Frames that follow the shape of your eyebrows are often more flattering than those that give you a second, differently shaped eyebrow look.

- **Very** large glasses are not classic, nor are **very** small glasses. Each can give you an eccentric, trendy, funky, yet sometimes interesting look—make sure it's an image you want.

- **Very** small glasses that have tiny lenses that barely cover your eyes can possibly make your eyes look closer together and even sometimes give you a cross-eyed look.

- If you choose to wear frames that are more substantial—thicker frames versus a thin metallic frame for example—it's often best if the frame follows, and covers, your eyebrows so that you won't have a thick, double-eyebrow look.

- Avoid glasses that droop down on the cheek, angling toward your jaw line—they can create a down-line that can make you look tired and old.

&⟋ Most of you are going to automatically avoid glasses that have any fancy detailing anywhere on them, but especially check out the bridge across your nose. If there is any detail on the bridge (or if it is a short bridge) it can definitely draw attention to your nose and can make your eyes look closer together as well as make your nose look big or strangely shaped. Also, for more classic and versatile looks, avoid thick bridges.

&⟋ Avoid detailing and/or a contrasting color on the temples (the arms).

&⟋ *Please* avoid lenses that are tinted rosy, yellowish, amber, bluish, greenish, or any other color that gives your skin a bruised look or strange coloration under and around your eyes.

Somehow, glasses and intelligence have become so intertwined—probably having something to do with nerds becoming *cool*—that men are buying glasses without prescriptions. With or without, here are some details that will help you pick out *smart* frames:

&⟋ A simple, elegant, versatile metal frame, or half frame, that gives the illusion of being your hair color or your skin tone is worth considering.

&⟋ Solid-color metallics (all gold or all silver for example) are more versatile and classic than colors such as blue or red.

&⟋ If your skin tone is golden, or your hair has golden highlights, your best metallics will have golden tones.

&⟋ Silver-toned frames can work well with ivory and pink skin tones and platinum, ash blond, ash brown, silver (gray), or white hair colors.

&⟋ Copper tones look nice on men with red or auburn hair.

&⟋ If you look best in toned down colors, select soft-tone metallics instead of those that are bright and shiny.

&⟋ If you look best in bright colors select a brighter metallic, avoiding those that look tarnished or dull.

&⟋ The new plastics are getting better and better looking—just make sure you don't look like you are wearing those from the '50s unless they are part of your *signature* vintage style.

&⟋ Avoid black frames if black isn't a flattering clothing color on you. Any frame in a color other than a neutral makes a definite statement—ask yourself if it is one that you are after.

⊘ **Bad Advice:** Heavy-set men should wear rectangular shaped frames to offset their chubby face.

① **My Advice:** Men of all sizes and shapes have different shaped faces not all full-bodied men have round, chubby faces, and besides, the stark contrast of a rectangular frame can call attention to any round face. Men with round faces may just want to avoid *round* frames.

Tortoise shell frames appear more casual than metallics and may not work well with your dressiest business attire. Your most flattering tortoise tones will be a combination of your skin tone, hair colors (beige, camel, brown), and perhaps black (if it looks good on you). They are best kept for more casual suits and business casual attire and only then **if** you are wearing colors and color combinations that work well with the colors in the glasses. If you only have one pair of glasses, avoid the limitations of tortoise or other more casual looks.

For sunglasses, keep all of the same size, shape, and color information in mind. Avoid shades that are reminiscent of "Men in Black," and those that are mirrored, with classic business looks. Please remember to take off your dark glasses when you are speaking with someone. It's very disconcerting to try to have a conversation with a person whose eyes you cannot see.

 **CLOAK WITHOUT A DAGGER**

JUST THE BASICS

⚔ Buy for your climate.

⚔ Select styles that go with the attire you wear to work.

⚔ Solid colors in your most commonly used neutrals.

⚔ Large enough to fit comfortably over a jacket.

⚔ Mid-calf length or longer is more sophisticated and practical.

BEYOND THE BASICS

Are you making a negative "arrival and departure" statement? Your coat needs to make a good impression because it is often your first impression, your last impression, and sometimes your only impression.

Select coats in styles and colors that go with your business and business casual attire, keeping your climate in mind. The more **basic** your topcoat (dress coat), overcoat, and raincoat the more versatile you will find them (do not think boring). Here are some *easy elegance* guidelines:

ϟ   Great colors to consider are your most used neutrals and the color
    of the shoes you wear the most. Your hair color/hair highlight color,
    and darker versions of these colors can be considered as well.

ϟ   A solid color is more versatile.

ϟ   Coats for your dressier suits will be plain but elegant and fairly
    dark in tone like black, charcoal, or navy, for example, versus
    camel/beige/tan which are more casual colors. Dressier coats
    are made out of fabrics that are refined looking—generally wool,
    cashmere, or blends of the two, although some of the
    microfibers and sueded rayons can be considered.

ϟ   The most elegant and practical length is at least as long as
    mid-calf—a coat is supposed to keep you dry and/or warm,
    and that includes your trousers and your legs. Shorter coats
    that come to, or just below, the knee look less elegant.

ϟ   You will want all of your coats to fit with ease over your suits
    and jackets because it's difficult to sit or walk, let alone drive,
    when you feel stuffed in your coat.

ϟ   The most versatile coat has matching buttons—even buttons that
    are hidden when closed should match because they will show when
    you wear your coat open, which is probably most of the time.

ϟ   A basic coat is free of contrasting or sporty stitching, epau-
    lets, and tabs, allowing it to look appropriate over dressy as
    well as casual attire.

ϟ   If you belt your coat, *please* make sure that you don't look like a
    sausage—slight definition, fine—a sausage, no! Belting styles
    with large or obvious pockets below the belt adds to the concern.

ϟ   You can use a buckle as it was intended, or you can tie the
    belt as you would tie a belt on your bathrobe. If you tie or
    buckle your belt in the back, make sure that it doesn't drape
    down over your "bum."

ϟ   If you tend to wear your coat open a lot, single-breasted styles
    are often less cumbersome and more flattering than double-
    breasted styles.

A trench coat with a zip-out lining may be the only coat you need if you
live in a milder climate and don't feel/have the need for a dressier coat.
From a color perspective, tan/beige/camel (wear in your best shade) is

classic, but so are navy, black, and gray, which are dressier looking—something to keep in mind if you are often in a suit.

Adding Variety

Once you have your *basics*, you can add other coats in other colors and styles you love. For example, if your raincoat is dressy, you might want to add a classic trench. If the coat you already own is a dark neutral, consider adding a classic camel polo. If you need to add a dressier coat, consider a velvet-collared chesterfield in black, dark gray, or navy. Coats in patterns or weaves such as herringbones are not as versatile as solid colors because they only work well over suits and trousers that are in colors that match those in the coat.

Are outerwear jackets an option? Yes, those that are nice looking can be worn for business casual. Nice looking? It has quality fabric (could be leather, suede, corduroy, wool, microfiber) and makes the same statement as your business casual attire—picture a shorter version of the coats described above, long enough to cover your longest blazer or jacket.

If you need an outerwear jacket that is versatile, choose one that doesn't "blouse," like a bomber style, for example, because it needs to hang straight at the bottom to work over blazers/jackets. If you aren't wearing a blazer or jacket, one possible exception for creative business casual (but not classic business casual) is the historic leather bomber/flight jacket. A drawstring around the bottom, or the waist, renders any outerwear jacket very casual.

 STORMY WEATHER

JUST THE BASICS

- ▲ **Scarves:** Solid color or subtle pattern and color-perfect.

- ▲ **Hats:** Not a necessity but if you wear one, wear it as if you've worn one forever (I'm not talking about ski caps). Complimentary style and color for you and what you are wearing—take it off when you enter a building.

- ▲ **Gloves:** Avoid ski-slope and snow-shovel styles and fabrics—for classic business and business casual, wear lined leather.

- ▲ **Umbrellas:** Solid color, match your most used neutrals—carry one in good repair.

BEYOND THE BASICS
Scarves

When it's cold outside, many men don a warm scarf—sometimes without thought of the color combination they are creating with their suit or coat, let alone their own coloring. All of the same color principles that apply to your most flattering clothing colors and color combinations are applicable here. Cheery bright red scarves don't look that way on Color Types that are more flattered by toned down colors—any bright color can make these Color Types look overly pale, anemic, and like they had better get in out of the cold and into bed.

If you live in a climate that calls for a warm scarf at the neck nearly daily for two or three months, consider treating yourself to one or two that are exceptional in color and quality—your scarf, after all, is part of your first and last impression.

The *easy, elegant* way to wear a warm scarf: fold in half so that both ends are together. Wrap around your neck and pull the ends through the fold and tuck the ends in the front of your coat or jacket. Can you still do it the way Snoopy did when he was fighting the Red Baron? Of course, just wrap the scarf around your neck and toss one end over your shoulder.

Hats

They are wonderful classics and they still serve a terrific purpose, but they can turn heads because so few men wear them anymore. If it sounds like something you would like to do, you can help bring them back into style. How? Simply by wearing them—they could end up being your *signature statement*. Yes, you can still tip your hat when approaching a woman on the sidewalk—just don't wear it tipped back on your head. Baseball caps and ski caps are classic also—on the weekend and on the ski slopes and for playing in or shoveling snow.

Hat styles, of course, need to compliment the shape of your face and, without seeing each of you in varying styles, it's hard to give advice. One thing I can say is that if your face is long or an oval that tends to look long, avoid hats with high crowns and small brims.

Since you are training your eye, go to a hat department or hat store and try them on—don't forget to check yourself from the side.

Gloves

Socks and gloves have two things in common. Both keep our extremities warm and both often end up with one of the pair missing. Worn now mostly for warmth and sports, your business gloves will be lined leather in your most used neutrals—consider matching your coat or the color of the shoes you wear most often. The warmest are lined in wool or cashmere and will fit you like a *glove*. They need to be long enough so you don't get a cold or inelegant gap between your glove and your sleeve.

Leather and suede gloves, unless they have sporty stitching or casual detailing, are dressier than those made of wool or microfibers. For business and business casual, please avoid those that look like you could wear them skiing or to shovel snow. No mittens, please.

Umbrella

Buy an umbrella large enough to keep the rain off you. I know that the smaller size is handier to carry and fine when it's just *raining,* but not at all useful when it comes to a downpour. Because most umbrellas are reasonably priced, make sure you always have one that is in good repair because if it isn't, you won't be making a good impression.

As far as color goes, most of you are probably thinking basic black, but if black isn't wonderful on you, consider matching the color of the shoes you wear most often or carry navy, dark gray, or brown. Solid colors with matching handles are businesslike and the most versatile.

SMALL DETAILS
WITH A BIG IMPACT ✉

STRESSING OUT ABOUT BEING OVER
OR UNDERDRESSED

JUST THE BASICS

- ♠ You can't be overdressed.

- ♠ Avoid being underdressed.

BEYOND THE BASICS

One of the things that happens when you look pulled together is that you appear more *dressed up,* even in your jeans. My advice is that you just get used to the fact that when you look super every day, people will notice and some will comment. It doesn't mean that you are overdressed—it probably means that they are underdressed.

Never wanting you to look less than your best, I still want you to be aware that there are times when you will want to be thoughtful about what you are going to wear when you want to accomplish something specific—the psychology of color and image. When you don't want to appear as powerful as you can, but you still don't want to look bad, wear less contrast (a gray suit with a blue shirt instead of a navy suit with a white shirt, for example) and a very classic subtle tie.

What about being underdressed? Since you are *now* in the habit of dressing well all of the time, when you find yourself in a situation where you appear underdressed, I'll assume that it really was an accident. You didn't think anything important was on your schedule when all of a sudden you have to sit in on a very crucial meeting in place of your boss. When this happens, your poise, self-confidence, easy, elegant business casual look and elegant attitude will get you through.

If you are invited to a business function after hours or on the weekend (including your co-workers' or boss's home) always inquire as to the dress—your significant other will be pleased at your thoughtfulness as well. When in doubt, overdress because you can always take your tie off.

TRAVELING IN STYLE

JUST THE BASICS

- Always look *elegant* and comfortable.

- No sweat or jogging suits.

- No sneakers.

- Dress for the person who is meeting you and/or what you're doing when you arrive.

BEYOND THE BASICS

How proud do you feel about telling your seat mate on a plane or train what you do when asked the inevitable question? Could he or she guess what you do by the way you are dressed? Yes. Would he or she guess executive, mid-level, entry-level, or unemployed?

What impression are you giving others about yourself and your company when you travel? Would they want to do business with you or your firm based on the way you look? Yes, you do reflect on your company's reputation as well as your own, every time you get dressed, whether you are going around the world or just around the corner.

Travel stylishly and comfortably—remember, comfort and sloppy are not synonyms. Select your travel attire according to your arrival activities and pretend that your seat mate may be the woman in your dreams, the president of your company, or the chairman of the major corporation you've been eager to work for.

If you are headed straight for a meeting or are being met by an associate, dress for business or business casual, depending on the circumstances. If you are traveling overseas, you may want to travel more casually—read casual elegance—and change into appropriate attire before you arrive.

Arrival and Departure Status

Although it would be nice, your luggage does not have to be the same brand or same style. But it should be the same color. Buy the best luggage you can afford in one of the hardy fabrics like canvas, nylon, or microfiber, with or without leather details, in one of your most used neutrals. Don't carry any luggage that looks like it won't make it through another trip—in other words, be proud to claim your bags, not embarrassed.

Packing It In

Some of you will end up traveling for business just once in a while, and some of you will travel constantly. Pick a color theme, such as navy and gray, navy and camel, black and gray, or black and camel, and you'll be able to pack easily. If you are taking/wearing a navy suit and you also need business casual attire, taking a pair of camel wool trousers to wear with your navy, gray, or black suit jacket and a good-looking shirt or sweater to dress down the suit gives you two different looks. If you are going to be away several days, add another suit and interchange all of the pieces.

Pack shirts and ties that you can wear with all of the different color combinations, as many as you need for as many days as you will be gone. Used to tie the colors together, your neck accessory **is critical** and the main reason you can coordinate your separates.

BEING GROOMED FOR VIP

JUST THE BASICS

- ◆ Light fragrance.

- ◆ Clean, short nails.

- ◆ Shower every morning.

- ◆ Use deodorant.

- ◆ Clean hair.

- ◆ Cleanly shaven or well trimmed beard/moustache.

- ◆ Fresh breath.

- ◆ No noticeable nose or ear hair.

BEYOND THE BASICS

Yes, some men need to be told to brush their teeth and/or use deodorant—even ambassadors. Mouthwash in the morning after brushing is a good idea, as is a sugarless mint or sugarless gum after meals.

Skin Care

There is nothing girly about wanting to have a **good complexion**. If you have good skin, I hope you know how blessed you are. It's difficult to look healthy and successful if your skin is peeling or acting up like you were a teenager. If you don't like the appearance of your skin, consult a dermatologist and/or a female friend who has knowledge in this area.

If you end up at the skin care counter of a department store, one of the most important things is finding someone who will work with you—someone who will give you samples to try *before* selling you a bottle or jar of something that may not work. A *smart tip*: Using too much moisturizer, or one that is too rich, can cause blemishes.

Hair Care

Women aren't the only ones who have bad hair days: More *smart tips*:

- Dirty or unkempt hair is not appropriate in any business situation.

- Spiked and highly gelled hair is fine if it looks *normal* or is expected in your business environment.

- If you are wearing your hair like you did when you were in high school or college, you might consider a more contemporary style for the image you want right now.

- Find a stylist that you can count on—*consistently* great haircuts are what you are after.

- A good cut is only as good as you can make it look on a daily basis—get one that you can manage.

- Always check the back of your head for "hair holes"—I believe that's a southern term most often used by women but it is equally as important for you because if someone sees the back of you first, he or she may never be interested in seeing the front. I'm not talking about a bald spot, but an unwanted parting of your hair sometimes caused by sleeping. For those of you who are bald, or going bald, it is much more elegant to slick your hair back than it is to comb it over a bald spot. Bald men can be very sexy—such as Sean Connery, Damon Wayans, and my "first" husband who was completely bald on top when I married him.

More men are having their hair highlighted—generally with blond streaks. If you are one of them, you need to be aware of the same concerns facing women who do the same. If your hair is brassy looking, it can sallow your skin and/or give you an "inexpensive" appearance. If your hair is too ash blond (gray blond), it can gray and dull your skin, giving you the opposite of a healthy look by causing you to look washed-out or sallow.

When it comes to classic business, your hair color is critical to your image and if the color is wrong it can really diminish your overall appearance, even if everything else is perfect. Find a good colorist—not necessarily the same person who cuts or styles your hair.

No obvious roots of a different color—**no exceptions**—even though you see this look on MTV. If you are not going to keep up your color or highlighting, *please* don't color or highlight in the first place.

Nails

No dirty or chewed-on nails or ripped cuticles at any place of business, **ever**. Using hand lotion a couple of times a day will help keep your cuticles and hands from getting dry. Hand lotion? For a guy? I've never seen a bottle of hand lotion that said, "For girls only."

Eyebrows

If you don't want to look like you are scowling, brush/comb your eyebrows "up." Bushy long eyebrows are some men's pride and joy—a personal *signature statement*. If you have them and they are so long that they come down to your eyelashes or way up on your forehead, consider trimming them a little for an interview, just as you would visible hairs in your nose or ears.

Fragrance

Please avoid wearing more than a hint of fragrance to work—strong fragrances are neither businesslike nor sexy. A person should be able to discern another's fragrance only when in very close proximity—fragrance is not applied by dumping some in your hand and slapping your cheeks. Ask an honest friend or co-worker if he or she can tell when you've entered the room and also be aware that some work environments have a fragrance-free policy.

MORE SMALL DETAILS WITH A BIG IMPACT

JUST THE BASICS

- Keep your million-dollar looks in good repair.

- Fix heels and shine shoes before they obviously need it.

- No loose threads.

- No stains.

- Don't over dry-clean your clothes.

- No shirts with wrinkled collar or cuffs.

- Don't chew gum.

- Use a real handkerchief to blow your nose.

- Transform your solid navy or black suit into dressy evening attire by wearing it with a white/soft white dress shirt and dressy tie.

BEYOND THE BASICS

Your image could be above reproach except for one small detail and it could be that detail for which you will be remembered.

Repairs

Keep your clothing and shoes in good repair. Wearing a garment or accessory that needs to be repaired can ruin your look—**please** don't do it. Train yourself to immediately repair, or have repaired, anything that needs it. Fix the heels on your shoes **before** they need it and shine them **before** they look like they need a shine. Replace shoelaces before they look frayed. Black magic marker works wonders on the edge of soles. Salt and/or chemicals that are used to melt ice can ruin your shoes and boots—get it off right away. Quality shoe manufacturers advise either using a 50/50 solution of water and vinegar or a de-salter that you buy in a shoe repair shop. I've found that a simple bottle of leather cleaner works well.

Please do not dry-clean your clothes to death—it really does kill them. — JoAnna

---

Dry Cleaning and Laundering

Before you take a garment to be dry-cleaned, first, try to remove "stuff" with a soft bristle brush. If that doesn't work, try a small amount of club soda on a clean, dry white cloth. Dry-cleaning two or three times a season is enough unless you spill something you can't get out on your own. In between cleanings, use your brush, particularly on the shoulders, lapels, sleeve and trouser cuffs, and under the arms.

Pressing adds more damage (and usually shine), so steaming is what to request. Jacket lapels, especially, should never be *pressed*. Take dry-cleaner plastic off your suits, jackets and pants the minute you get them home and hang them on proper wooden hangers (the curve in the hanger goes from the back of the neck, forward).

Ask your best clothing stores who they recommend for dry-cleaning suits and laundering shirts—note that they may not be the same establishment. When you remove your jacket, hang it—no, not on the back of a chair. At home, hang it where air can circulate around it—in the closet is fine but not in a cramped closet. In a perfect world, every man would have a valet—not a manservant, a wooden valet. Treat your jacket well and it will pay you back for years to come.

I know men who loathe taking their shirts to the laundry because at least one comes back unwearable with wrinkles and chipped or missing buttons. Starch can cut the life of a shirt, so consider alternating no starch with light starch.

If you work for a bank, credit union, or brokerage firm and you're wearing a shirt with a missing or chipped button (yes, someone will notice), the message is: He doesn't care about the way he looks, so he *might not be* careful with my money, my future. All you were guilty of was not taking the time to change your shirt, but that simple act could cost you or your company a client (who could refer other clients, who could in turn refer other clients, and so on).

Keep a sewing kit and extra collar stays handy at home, at work, and in the car. Yes, you can sew on a button. Also keep one lint roller (it has sticky tape on it) at home and another in your desk—it's much more effective than most lint brushes. If you own a dog who rides in your car, keep another roller in the car.

Tidy Up Loose Ends

Keep an eye out for loose threads—trim them right away because they can make even an expensive garment look *less*. Keep scissors handy where you dress and in your desk at work to trim small threads—it is amazing, but lack of attention to detail of this kind sends a message that you are careless or, perhaps worse, unaware. Never pull a loose thread, especially on a button. A few small dangling threads on a garment is not necessarily a sign that it was poorly made—but a lot of loose threads could be. Look all new items over carefully before wearing them for the first time and trim as needed. Always open all of your pockets—carefully, because you could cut the fabric. If your vision isn't perfect, put on your "readers" before you cut even your first thread.

Protect Against Moths

If you have even the tiniest possibility of being "hit" with moths, take precautions. **Cedar chests, cedar-lined closets, cedar balls, or cedar blocks do not kill moths.** Use only moth blocks or balls that say right on the package that they **kill** moths and their larva. It's fine to use a cedar chest, cedar closet, or garment bag *if* you add this protection. When it's time to wear these clothing items again, you can air them out by hanging them on the shower rod for a day or two—air needs to circulate around them. Sweaters can be put in the dryer on "fluff" (no heat) with some fabric softener sheets.

Light-weight wool items that you wear during the summer months need to be shaken well or brushed every few weeks. Clothes that have been dry-cleaned are **still** susceptible to moths.

It's Not *Smart* to Chew

I'm talking about gum because the *other* is too obvious. Unless you are alone and not on the phone, no gum please. It looks unprofessional and inelegant. Also, it can be distracting and a major irritant to others—especially if you are popping it.

The Elegance of Using a *Real* Handkerchief

Always using a *real* handkerchief—clean, of course—instead of those you pull out of a box makes a very good impression on both men and women. Once stained beyond the laundry's repair, throw them away.

Dressy Evenings

Getting ready for dressy evening business and social functions is a breeze—just transform your navy, black, or dark gray suit by wearing it with an exceptional white or soft white shirt and a very dressy-looking silk tie. This look will take you anywhere except black tie or white tie.

By the way, when wearing a cummerbund with a tuxedo, the pleats open upwards (to hold theater tickets). Tuxedo trousers have a plain cuff (no cuff). For the most classic, understated look (and if you want timeless photos), wear a white tuxedo shirt, pleated, or plain front, and a black tie, and cummerbund. I have a picture of William (the first) and me taken at a White House dinner—he's wearing a coral ruffled tux shirt that had a tiny edging of black on the ruffles. You can guess about what year it was taken by the style and color of his shirt.

Boxers Versus Briefs

What would a men's wardrobe book be without a discussion of boxers or briefs. Men are lucky—they generally don't have to worry about VPL (visible panty line) unless they wear their pants too tight. Longer, wider leg boxers are not appealing to most women (just in case you wanted to know) and they generate a lot of extra fabric to tuck down your pant legs. Shorter, narrower legged boxers are far better looking. After that, it's all a matter of opinion and personal preference.

One evening at a reception in New York I was talking shop with an interesting man—one of the owners of a famous magazine that had featured my company, Color 1 Associates. We were discussing an article on men's underwear that I had just written for the newspaper, and he told me that he was so paranoid (his word) about color-coordinating his attire that when he has shirts made, he has short leg boxers made to match. No, I'm not suggesting that you need to do the same, but I will say that if you have any dingy white pedestrian looking briefs I hope you will toss them out now. Yes, even if they don't have any holes in them—we don't find them appealing! To read this article, visit www.dressingsmart.com and click on *"Smart Wardrobe."* Own enough clean boxers/briefs that you can go two weeks without having to do the laundry.

Husbands and Dads Can be Really Neat and Interesting Men, Too

Some men wonder why their significant other takes them for granted and why there sometimes seems to be a respect issue with the children. Often, your younger significant others don't have a clue as to who you really are, how very good you are at your job and how admired you are by others. They probably think that you're a special dad but they don't know that you are also a special *person*. They just think of you as Dad, instead of a *really neat guy*. Perhaps she thinks the same. Could it be because most of the time you spend with them, your image is less than wonderful? Less than good? Even less than okay?

Color-perfect (for you), comfortable, washable *bases,* and jeans with good-looking T-shirts/shirts and sweaters are the answer to looking good when you're "off-duty." If they are comfortable they take away any excuse for not looking great ALL OF THE TIME. *Please* toss your grubbies so you won't be tempted to wear them ever again. Okay, you can keep something for painting or working on the car. Denims, khakis, and corduroy that have a touch of lycra or spandex in them add tons of comfort in the pants arena. No sloppy looks, please. Remember that sloppy and comfort are not synonyms.

DOES YOUR PERCEPTION
OF YOURSELF MATCH
OTHERS' PERCEPTION OF YOU?

JUST THE BASICS

- ♣ In the mind of another person, you are what he or she thinks you are.

- ♣ Make sure your image is sending the message you want to be received.

BEYOND THE BASICS
It's very difficult to look at yourself objectively—it's almost as if you have become immune to yourself, if you feel that:

- ○ Your favorite (shiny and somewhat threadbare at this point) special occasion suit still looks great.

- ○ The navy blazer you wore all through college still fits you, even though you are ten pounds heavier.

- ○ You don't receive compliments on a regular basis.

⊘ You lament that you can't attract the type of women (or any women) that you would like—**it's definitely time to change your image.**

The idea is to have the image you want match the image you create and have that match the image, or message, that's received. Sorry for the convoluted sentence. I'll give it another try.

If you think you are sending one message and a different one is being received, either you aren't on the same wavelength (your boss OR "that" woman on the 6th floor wouldn't notice you no matter what) or you aren't sending the message you think you are.

It's hard to see yourself as others see you. Perhaps to be more objective and analytical about your look, take a picture of yourself and study it as you do when you study yourself in the mirror. When you want to check out or change the message your image is sending, your friends and family may not be your best resource for objectivity because they are *used* to you. Change can be unnerving because the "old" you has a certain familiarity and comfortableness.

Do people really notice when you start looking better? When I was working with private clients, a congressman's office was filled with my devotees, including the congressman and his wife. When new staff members joined this office, they were *talked into* seeing me for a consultation. While I was working with one new "convert," he mentioned that when a staff member would come into work in the morning, she/he would create a buzz—what someone was wearing would be defined as a "B.J." or an "A.J."—something they had "before JoAnna" or something they bought "after JoAnna."

As you begin to look *different* you will carry yourself differently—you will have more *presence* and heads will turn. When you first realize that people are turning to look at you, you may wonder if your fly is open.

DEVELOPING A *SIGNATURE* STYLE

JUST THE BASICS

■ Find a way to subtly set yourself apart.

■ Individuality is always in style.

BEYOND THE BASICS

If you desire to be unique, to truly set yourself apart from other men, you'll want to learn to transform the same (or slightly different) clothes other men are wearing into your own distinctive *signature statement*.

Why did I say the "same" clothes other men are wearing? Because you're all wearing the uniform look of suits, blazers/jackets, trousers, shirts, and ties—so it's harder to appear different (special).

Why consider a *signature statement*? Because it can subtly tie you to everyone you work with/for and others you come into contact with on a regular basis (the person who seats you at your favorite restaurant for lunch, your pharmacist, grocer, barber, salesperson where you shop for clothes, and so on). In an interesting and pleasant way, you will be noticed.

To be noticed is to be remembered; to be remembered opens doors. Co-workers who normally wouldn't take the time may even make sure they get to see you every day so they can see what you are wearing. When they need someone on their team, you may come to mind. When you need a prescription filled extra fast, your pharmacist knows who you are. When your favorite restaurant is crowded, you will be seated. When new neckties come in that have some purple in them, or have dots, your salesperson will call you. Purple or dots? Read on—you can be appropriately attired and still look unique.

What could your *signature* be? Anything you want it to be. Here are some ideas:

- Always wear braces, both new and vintage—collect them to go with all of your suits, jackets, shirts, and ties.

- Always wear a tie tack or a tie bar—collect them, both antique and new.

- Always wear variations of the same color—every day. That means when you open your closet, all you will see is gray—for example, gray suits, jackets, and trousers, except for your shirts, which can be in any of the colors you like, and the ties, which will all have gray in them but will generally contain other colors as well, like the colors of your shirts. Substitute for gray the color of your choice. All the shades of gray (or blue if that's the color you choose) need to be from the same color family and will be lighter and darker versions of each other. When you shop for new ties, you can ignore all ties that don't have at least a touch of gray in them.

- Always wear ties that have purple in them—you get to choose your own *signature* color, but every day your tie will have a touch of that color. If you are wearing a navy suit with a blue shirt, your tie will have navy, blue (that matches your shirt), and purple. It could have other colors as well.

- Always wear ties with dots—little dots, medium-size dots, and maybe—depending on your place of work, the color combination, and your Color Type—larger dots. You can choose a different pattern (stripes, for example), but each day you will have on a tie with the same pattern. When you shop, you will save a lot of time just zeroing in on your *signature* pattern—at a glance you can tell if there are any ties you might want.

- Always wear a vintage tie.

- Always wear an extraordinary, perfect white or soft white shirt—find them in different textures and weaves. Only wear ties, suits, and jackets that will work well with the same white as the shirt.

- Always wear a vest.

- Always wear a hat to and from work—don't forget to tip it and take it off when you enter a building (it's not cold or rainy inside). What good does it do you then? It will still be in your hand—still part of who you are.

- Always wear French cuffs with links from your collection of old and new.

- Wear different watches from your collection—picking out each day the one that goes the best with what you are wearing.

- Always wear a bow tie—no clip-ons or pre-tied, please.

- Always wear a flower in your lapel. There is some disagreement as to the proper flowers but generally a rosebud, carnation, blue cornflower, or daffodil are fine. There is also some disagreement as to the propriety of wearing a flower and a pocket square at the same time so I guess that comes down to personal preference—mine is to wear one at a time.

There are those among you who may find wearing a *signature statement* boring, but others of you may have just found your answer to *easy elegance*. Are some of you worried about being noticed for the wrong reasons? You can **stand out** without *standing out*.

Your desire for individuality or for wanting to do it YOUR way won't shoot you in the foot if you don't wear something like a black leather jacket with zippers, sneakers, T-shirts with designs or sayings, shorts or short pants, spiked green hair, or white socks at the wrong time.

Will people think that you are eccentric? Depending on your *signature*, maybe a few. *Smile.* Others won't even realize what you are doing—they'll just think that you look super all the time. Most people will think you are a very attractive and *interesting* man.

If anyone gets verbal with you about it, you can either share this book with them (a very gracious act) or ignore them and let them continue to muddle through, keeping their hit and miss habit of looking good one day and not so good the next.

BUILDING FROM ZERO OR PARING DOWN

JUST THE BASICS

The following ideas are for you if you:

- Don't have much or anything at all appropriate to wear.

- Feel your wardrobe seems out of control.

- Feel overwhelmed.

- Just don't know what to buy or how to start.

- Are on a tight budget.

- Or simply prefer a minimal wardrobe.

BEYOND THE BASICS

When you have a balanced wardrobe, you don't have to think about having the right thing to wear.

- Build your entire wardrobe around a *signature* color.

- Buy only *basics* and *classics*—uncomplicated, but elegant.

- Wear *bases* with your suit jackets, blazers, and odd jackets for business casual, or nice shirts or sweaters (without a tie) with your suits.

- Wear only black or brown shoes depending on your *signature* color, and/or how dressed up you need to be for work.

- Match your shoes to your belt.

- Make a choice between gold-toned/brass and silver and own only one belt with that color buckle, one watch, and cufflinks that only look good with your choice.

- Match your briefcase/laptop bag, umbrella, luggage, and wallet to your shoes and belt.

- Non-"fat" leather wallet, only—no canvas or velcro.

- Consider owning two pairs of shoes, a lace-up and a slip-on, both in your chosen color so you'll have a change of pace.

- As much as possible, buy only garments that can be worn year-round in your climate.

CLOSET SURGERY 🚑

JUST THE BASICS

🚑 For *easy elegance*, get your wardrobe organized. *NOW.*

BEYOND THE BASICS

How would you like to leave the house every morning feeling dynamite about the way you look, never giving it a second thought no matter what you might end up doing that day? Even having an unexpected meeting with the president of your firm wouldn't rattle you.

It's often said, but not always true, that you should give away those items of clothing you haven't worn for one year. It is true that *easy elegance* is more easily achieved when your closet isn't full of stuff you can't or shouldn't wear, but there may be something that you aren't wearing because you don't know how to utilize it. For a stress-free experience every morning, **get organized now.**

Is this elective minor surgery or major mandatory surgery? It depends on you and your closet, but if you desire a brand new *you*, you may need to operate on, amputate, and transplant things in your closet. Before surgery, get a good mental picture of the man you want to be, what he looks like, and your lifestyle. Steady your hand and begin—it doesn't have to be painful.

Your goal should be to dress easily in the morning without stress, then go on about your day without having to give the way you look another thought. The following should help you achieve this goal.

Step 1
Remove everything from your closet(s)—
work in natural daylight.

Step 2
Evaluate each garment and separate your clothing
into three piles.

Pile #1: Those items that are worn out, hopelessly stained, you hate, the wrong size now and probably forever will be, uncomfortable or scratchy, just don't look good on you, and you haven't worn in a long time.

Take a second look at all of these things. Can you figure out why you hate something? Is there anything about it that you could change that would make you like it—make it useful? If trousers are uncomfortably tight, can they be altered?

Perhaps a jacket you think you don't care for just needs to be paired with a different shirt and/or pair of trousers. Are those things you haven't been wearing out of style—like an old sack suit that now looks too boxy? Could a little tailoring give it a new silhouette? For the time being, put these items in pile #2 or #3.

If your weight goes up and down, store (someplace other than your main closet, if possible) things you love that will possibly be useful in the future. Give away anything you feel another person could use, and toss the rest. Can't stand to give away or toss an old treasured item? Put it someplace where you can go and visit it.

Pile #2: Those garments that you like but require mending, tailoring, or cleaning. Handle these chores as soon as possible.

Pile #3: Clothing you feel good in; things you like but aren't terrific colors for you; and garments you would like to wear more often if only you had more things that went with them.

For those items that are not a good color or the right clarity for you, figure out if you can save them by wearing them with a color-perfect shirt, tie, or sweater. If not, they go in your giveaway pile. Should you keep them to wear when nothing *special* is going on? My advice is to give them up unless it means you'll be going naked. You will never feel good about the way you look in them and the days you wear them will definitely not be special.

Now it's time to look at those garments you would love to wear more often if only you had (fill in the blank) to go with them. Make a list of things you will need to purchase to accomplish this. If you want to take the items shopping with you, as soon as you finish step #3, you can put them in a bag and *get going.* Do I sound determined to get you organized?

Step 3
Coordinate your outfits and take notes.

First, if you need several business casual looks, how many *bases* can you make? If you'd love to make more bases, add to your shopping list the colors of shirts/sweaters/trousers you'll need to accomplish this. Take your list and the pieces you're going to match with you—you know that the shade of the color needs to be the same, but the value of the color can be a little lighter or darker.

How many jackets do you have that will work over your bases or with separates you would like to combine? If you wear a lot of business casual, always keep your eye open for super odd jackets that will work well with the colors of trousers and shirts/sweaters you already have.

How many separates can you coordinate into interesting looks by tying them together with a necktie that has all of the colors of your jacket, shirt, and trousers? Add colors for ties to your shopping list. Don't forget that combining like values of colors—like two medium colors, for example—can create interesting looks. You may want to review page 125. Add the details to your list.

Remember that mental picture of the *new* you? Keeping it in mind, are there any holes in your closet? If most of your clothes are too casual to wear to the place you spend at least 40 hours a week, that's a **big** hole. Add needs and desires to your list—the needs will make your wardrobe work for you and the desires will help make your life work for you.

A desire? One man may have always wanted a cashmere blazer; another is always looking for another perfect white shirt; yet another is happy to go to flea markets with his significant other every weekend, just to see if he can find another pair of cufflinks or a vintage tie for his collection.

Step 4
Put your keepers back in the closet.

There is more than one good way to organize your closet, so whatever works best for you is the way to do it. The most popular way is by garment— a separate section each for suits, jackets, trousers, and shirts. Some men also like to hang ties that they have found work with a certain suit right around the neck of the jacket so they don't have to hunt for it in their morning fog. The most convenient tie racks are those that are horizontal versus vertical because you can see more of the tie. Use good wooden hangers for suits and jackets—the investment will pay you back by keeping your clothing in good shape. Also, wire hangers weren't meant for knit shirts.

Placing square containers on top of your closet shelf, with the opening facing you, is a good way to keep everything else (sweaters, knit shirts, jeans) organized and in full view—the top of the containers gives you a second shelf.

Small shelves for your shoes (versus those pointy metal things) are fabulous. You'll never regret the investment—buy them at one of the big linen or hardware stores in the closet department. Count how many shoes you have before you go (include your athletic shoes) so you'll know how many shelves to get. They can be stacked so that you can get several into a small space— try placing them on the floor of your closet under your shirts or jackets.

Make your closet(s) as light-filled as possible. Unfortunately, many men have to deal with peering into dark closets, trying to decipher colors, especially whether the garment is black or a very dark navy. If you have this concern, separate black and navy suits and jackets with one of another color. This simple act can it save you numerous trips to the window or a lamp. Do the same with your socks.

Some men feel that they can more easily manage their wardrobe if they write down each coordinated look so they can refer to their notes to keep them on track. For one client, a lawyer, I put subtle Roman numerals on the label of each suit jacket, blazer, and odd jacket. Numbers were placed on his ties (1, 2, 3

4, etc.) on the inside of the small end, and letters on his shirt labels (in indelible ink). All white shirts had the letter A , for example, soft whites were B, blues of the same shade were C— you get the picture. Trousers were simply described as gray, navy, camel, black, and so on.

The notebook I prepared for him had every good look, by suit or jacket. He would get up in the morning, go to his closet and decide which suit or jacket he wanted to wear that day. Checking his book, under that suit or jacket (matching Roman numerals), he would read, for example, shirt A with ties 1, 7, and 10, or shirt C with ties 2, 7, and 12. (Tie 7 has both white and blue in it.) Written under jacket IV he would find gray trousers, shirt B, with ties 4 and 14, for example.

Some of you may be thinking, "Couldn't he figure this out for himself?" He is really, really smart in several other ways and, after all, this isn't his field of expertise. Still a little obsessive, you think? Not for him—it made his life so *easy* and he felt like he looked *elegant* every day. Just one thing less for him to worry about—that's one of the things he is very smart about—delegating responsibility. Keeping him on track with his wardrobe was my responsibility.

As you wear each look that you put together for the first time, mentally evaluate how you feel in it. Was it a million-dollar look? Or would you try it with a different tie next time? Training your eye is a process. If you are a notebook/journal kind of guy, make notes next to outfits—perhaps a plus or a minus so you are reminded to work on those that don't measure up to your new higher standards.

YOU'RE GOING SHOPPING? REALLY?

JUST THE BASICS

- If you are in a hurry, go immediately to page 152 and review the *Just the Basics: A Quick Reference.*

- Think quality instead of quantity.

- Take your list.

- Don't shop when you are tired, in a hurry, or hungry.

BEYOND THE BASICS

Some men like to shop and some men hate it. Reasons for hating it range from feeling out of place in what they consider is a woman's venue, being "forced" to shop when they would rather be watching a game, to simple, truthful lack of interest. You don't need to like to shop to end up looking super every day—you only need to know what looks exceptional on you. And, it can save a lot of time if you also know what doesn't, because you can zero in on only the best.

Invest in a wardrobe that works for you by making each purchase count— a well planned wardrobe will take you anywhere in the world. Before you invest in any garment or accessory, ask yourself if it will serve you well in your workplace, with your lifestyle, and help you create the exact look you want **right now**.

Learn how to build a *smart wardrobe* that works for you—one that you can count on, one that makes you feel super every day, one that you love— one that you can **manage**.

If you are going to start a new job in a new industry (or it's your first job), before you shop you might want to research the expected attire in your field and then, if you are on a budget, go shopping in your own closet first. Do you have pieces that you can build on? A navy suit? A nice pair of gray trousers? A navy blazer for classic business casual? If you don't have a clue what your personal style should be, don't worry—it will define itself as you go and you will find that an *easy, elegant* wardrobe will take you anywhere with confidence.

My friend Phyllis brought a friend with her to Washington to shop with me—the friend had just gotten divorced and was in need of both an "uplifting" experience and an "update" of her wardrobe. She had enough business suits for her executive look, but she needed *date* clothes.

We went to our favorite off-price store, and, after about a half-hour of collecting things for both of them to try on, I put them in a larger dressing room where all of the women undress and try on in full view of everyone else. I kept going in and out, bringing more things for them to try.

On one of my trips in, a woman came over and asked me where I was finding the clothes I was bringing in. Phyllis said, "She's shopping off the same racks you are." One of the reasons we were causing such a stir, and why everyone was watching us, was because I was only having them try on clothing that would look good on them from a color standpoint—their best shades, clarity, and color combinations. And, of course, from a style perspective, I only brought in super looking "stuff." The result was that they looked wonderful in almost everything.

Shopping with a trained eye makes all the difference. Armed with all of these *smart tips,* I'm sure you're going to be successful and have more fun, as well. Well, maybe. Here are some reminders:

 Take your list of anything you need that will complete, accessorize, or pull together something you already have.

■ Wear something you like and are comfortable in, even a plain, *nice* T-shirt and jeans if you are shopping for business casual. If you are looking for suits and you always wear a white shirt, wear one when shopping.

■ If you are shopping for suits or trousers, wear the type of shoes that you plan to wear with what you're looking for.

■ Don't shop when you are tired, hungry, or in a hurry.

■ Keep focused but keep an open mind—even when you're shopping with a list, you may find something unexpected. If you are uncertain about something and it's returnable, take it home and try it on again the next day to see if it fits the "you" you want to be.

■ When you are attempting to change the way you look, avoid shopping with a friend who might cast doubt on what you are trying to accomplish. Once you are more sure of your new-found knowledge and know how successfully it is working for you (lots of compliments) you can shop with anyone and not be swayed by their comments—**you** will be handing out the advice.

■ Superb looks can be found in any price range. Forget about labels and pretend that you are in a foreign country and you don't have a clue as to the prestige level of the store or brand. Unless you have an endless supply of money, think inexpensive chic—shop for style, quality, comfort, and price. I know that some of you get your self-assurance from a label, but when you are truly confident that you look fabulous, you will love knowing that you didn't need a designer or brand name to make a million-dollar look.

■ Don't get hung up on the size marked on a label or on the size marked on the racks you are shopping from. Learn to eyeball a garment and you can most always tell if it will work for you without looking at the size. When I have time, I check every size. You'll be surprised at what neat things you will find in the wrong sizes that will fit you—your size 42 long might be hanging on the 40 regular rack and some styles of jackets in other sizes and lengths just might be perfect.

■ Whatever you buy, when you get it home, coordinate it with existing items and try everything on. You may have seen women doing this—it works as well for men. If you still don't have the look **YOU** want, return it. If you did just create a new look that will bring you self-assurance and admiring glances, make a mental note of it or write it down. Start wearing it immediately—don't save it unless you have a specific meeting coming up where it will make its debut.

> Don't buy anything that isn't equal to, or better than, the best look you have right now. — JoAnna

One of my sisters, a Color 1 Associate, and a charming guy friend of hers came out for a visit from the Northwest. He said he needed a few new things, particularly some jeans, but he hated to shop and only wanted to spend a max of a half-hour. First, we plied him with a wonderful breakfast, then we took him to the *dreaded* mall. In a half-hour he had several new pairs of jeans and some great shirts. He didn't want to leave, and he said that it was the best time he had ever spent in a mall......Of course, it didn't hurt that he had the full attention of two women who knew exactly what colors and styles would give him a million-dollar look.

Stores sell different merchandise depending on where in the country they are located. In Washington, DC, for example, more men buy conservative suits so a mass market store may not stock as many suits and jackets with side vents, since some stores still consider them up-fashion. From a bottom-line standpoint, they prefer to keep their money in inventory that sells all of the time (center vent, 2- and 3-button suits) instead of stocking for customers with diverse tastes.

Keep in mind that salespeople have their oddities (too) and that their advice and comments may not be true for you. After all, they don't know who you are or who you desire to be, and their advice, especially when it comes to color, may be inaccurate. I am grateful to many salespeople for their helpfulness and caring, and it would be nice if they had color and wardrobe training so they could help clients even more, but few do. **YOU** need to take control of your most flattering colors, clarity, and color combinations. It also helps to keep in mind that mental picture of the way you would like to look.

In the beginning, don't shop with someone who can influence you—even your wife or best friend. You are shopping for the image you want, not anyone else's. You may have heard it before. You hold something up and say, "What about this?" And the other person says, "That doesn't look like you. You aren't shopping for the old you."

Looking important is far better than looking like you don't have a clue, but looking great is completely different from acting self-important. Some say that the more expensive the suit, the more power it gives you. I say that if you train your eye to understand what colors and color combinations are flattering to you, it's possible to shop literally anywhere and look better than a guy who doesn't have this knowledge—no matter how much he is able to spend on his clothes. You can get good and great quality labels, including designer, at super prices—you just have to be willing to put in the time to find them. Before you go looking for them, it will help to train your eye if you try on a jacket that is more expensive than you can afford just to find out how it feels and hangs.

> A well dressed man is never out of style, and you don't need to look like a male model on a runway in New York, Los Angeles, Paris, London or Milan to be considered very well dressed. — JoAnna

PAYING THE PRICE $

JUST THE BASICS

$ If you are on a budget, find the best prices for all clothing items at off-price, outlet, and discount stores.

$ For major retailers, mark sale dates on your agenda, and if you are a hard-to-fit size, shop early.

BEYOND THE BASICS

What can you expect to pay for a good-looking suit? Depending on where you shop, you will pay as little as $109 to $149 for top brands (including some designers) at outlet and off-price stores and starting at $495 in a quality department store. Sometimes men's stores will run specials where you can buy two suits for about $500. What's the price of the most expensive suit made? I don't know the answer, but I did visit a store (for research purposes) whose suits ranged in price from $2,500 to $5,000 and I do know of tailor-made (bespoke) suits that sell for $10,000—not something that I personally aspire for you to spend your money on! If you want good quality for less, shop the sales in your better stores and always keep your eye open for super finds in off-price stores and outlets. A wonderful odd jacket or suit can be had for 50% to 70% off the last price marked.

What's the difference between suits that are less expensive and those that cost more? The difference is in the details, the suit and lining fabric, and the construction—especially in the amount of hand stitching in the garment. More expensive suits can have, but don't always have, hand-stitched interfacing inside the chest and lapel (versus fused interfacing); silk lining; reinforced pockets; pockets that are lined further into the pocket in the same fabric as the suit; functioning buttonholes/handmade button-holes; and buttons that are sewn on by hand.

Some jackets (expensive ones) really do have working buttonholes on the sleeves. Depending on who you ask, you leave the first one or two open and, depending on who you talk to, they are wonderful or pretentious. Some men like to show that the suit they are wearing is higher end or custom-made. Others feel it's a bit pompous—an ego thing. Just like a monogram on a shirt, it's personal preference and I know elegant men in both camps.

The buttonhole in your jacket is for a pin or a flower. Any pins should be subtle and generally non-political, non-pro, or anti this or that. "Theme" pins and cufflinks should also be discreet for classic business and if there is a shadow of a doubt that they would ever offend someone, don't wear them.

Fused interfacings (the fabric or material that's placed between the out-side of a jacket and the lining), versus those that are hand-basted, can cause lapels and the chest area of jackets to bubble or ripple after dry-cleaning. Although getting better, some fusing materials still interact with dry cleaning chemicals and, if they do, this rippled look cannot be corrected. Ask your salesperson if the jacket you are considering will give you this problem. If he/she tells you, "no problem," and you end up with bubbles/ripples, take the suit or jacket back to to the store where you purchased it. Hand-basting (and all hand stitching) adds to the cost of a jacket so, in general, a better made suit will not have fused interfacings.

There seems to be a rumor going around that a fully sewn down lining is not a good thing. It's fine. And it has been "forever" rumored that unlined and half-lined jackets are a sign of poor quality. Untrue—as a matter of fact, it involves more work because all of the inside seams need to be finished perfectly.

In a quality patterned suit, all patterns must align, or match, everywhere—at pockets, flaps, seams, and lapels. Also check the armholes to make sure the seam is smooth without apparent gathering or puckering.

Can you order extra sizes? Some stores have up to size 54 extra tall on the floor and extra sizes can be "made to measure," depending on the manufacturer. Sometimes you can order an extra pair of pants—something to consider if you tend to wear them out before your jackets.

What does a designer label add to the price? Often a lot of money and, for some men, prestige and self assurance from the label. A mind-set.

Seeking Counsel ← Help

Just the Basics

◆ To take the guesswork out of which colors and color combina-tions are best for **you**, visit www.DressingSmart.com for the phone number of the Color 1 Associate, International Image and Style Consultant, closest to you.

◆ Not all image consultants are authorities when it comes to personal color.

BEYOND THE BASICS

Why am I recommending Color 1? Because they have had the best training available anywhere in the world.

An interesting and informative consultation with one of them will result in your being in charge of your best colors and color combinations—forever. They can also help you build the perfect *smart wardrobe* for your current job or for the career move you would like to make. If there is not yet an Associate near you, there are excellent color charts on our website that will help you with all of your color decisions. You have to figure out your Color Type (a free online quiz will help you) so you will know which *Smart Chart* or *Mini Smart Chart* to order. There is also a print-out version of each chart available on the website.

Not all image consultants are experts in color. Some consultants who **DO** color charts have had only two or three hours of color training and little or no wardrobe training. Most of their approximate two-day training is on how to sell a woman makeup.

Color 1 Associates have studied approximately four weeks before their actual technical color training which lasts **six full days** and is followed by five additional days of advanced wardrobe training. An apprenticeship program continues their training. Flying in from all over the world, the Associates have invested up to $5,685 *plus* airfare, hotel, and dining expenses in their training versus the $250, or less, other companies charge for their two-day color (makeup sales) training.

JUST THE BASICS: A QUICK REFERENCE

An exceptional look is attained, in part, by paying attention to all of the "little" details that make up the total picture of you. This abbreviated *Just the Basics* checklist is also printed on the last page of the book so you can tear it out and take it shopping with you as a reminder that these small components are a huge consideration when it comes to looking great.

📖 **Mirror:** Use one that is full-length and check your front, side, and back views.

📖 **Your look:** Easy and elegant, professional yet stylish, perfect for your career and personal goals. Well coordinated, pulled together, totally elegant million-dollar look, whether strictly business or business casual.

📖 **All colors:** Great shades for you.

📖 **Clarity:** Not too bright and not too toned down for your specific coloring.

📖 **Color combination:** Not too strong or overpowering and not too weak or washed-out looking on you—again, perfect for your coloring.

📖 **Pattern size:** Perfect for your coloring.

📖 **Fit:** Well tailored for you; shoulder line a tiny bit wider than your hipline—creating a V shape that keeps you from looking stodgy.

📖 **Fabrics:** Natural fibers and blends of natural with a small percentage of other.

📖 **Jacket:** If classic styling, just covering your seat; sleeve length perfect, falling just below your wrist bone, allowing ¼" to ½" shirt cuff to show.

📖 **Shirt:** Impeccably pressed; not too big or too tight in the neck; not more than ½" cuff showing; no long pointed or extreme spread collars; collar points touch the body of your shirt when wearing a tie, no button-downs with dressy suits or ties.

📖 **Trousers:** Long enough to cover the heel of your shoe with at least a slight break so that you cannot see your socks even when you walk.

📖 **Tie:** Contains colors of suit or jacket, shirt, trousers; best clarity of colors for you; matches approximate width of jacket lapel; pattern size perfect for your color type; knot fits well with your collar style; tied no shorter than the top of your waistband and no longer than the bottom of your waistband; hangs in a straight line centered with your fly.

📖 **Shoes:** Smooth leather plain- or cap-toe lace-ups or dressy slip-ons; polished and well maintained; outstanding color for you and your attire; no penny loafers with dressy suits.

📖 **Socks:** Wear them—match shoes or trousers; over-the-calf length; no bold patterns that scream "look at me."

📖 **Belt:** Match shoes for *easy elegance*; solid color; plain smooth leather; about 1 ¼" to 1 ½" ; never worn with braces.

📖 **Braces:** Colors coordinate with shirt, tie, and suit or jacket; leather attachments match shoes; metal matches other metals you are wearing.

📖 **Handkerchief:** Clean and stain-free.

📖 **Pocket square:** Not necessary; solid color or pattern coordinates with shirt, suit or jacket, and tie but doesn't match tie exactly.

📖 **Watch:** Makes same statement as your attire—no sport watches with classic business or classic business casual.

📖 **Metals:** match belt buckle, cufflinks, blazer buttons, metal on braces, shoe buckles.

📖 **Ring:** One or none.

📖 **Other jewelry:** If in doubt, none for interview; minimal in most business arenas.

📖 **Briefcase/laptop bag:** Match most used shoe/belt color or your hair color.

📖 **Topcoat/raincoat:** wonderful color for you; darker colors are dressier; coordinates with your attire; at least mid-calf in length.

📖 **Hair:** Stylish and clean.

📖 **Facial hair:** Still possible prejudice depending on industry and the age group of the men in charge; safer to be clean shaven for interviews—then, well trimmed personal preference.

📖 **Other personal grooming:** Clean body; wear deodorant; clean teeth; fresh breath; clean clipped nails; no nose or ear hair showing.

📖 **Posture:** Good.

📖 **Train your eye:** Don't believe everything you see, read, or hear.

📖 **Comfort level:** Good or great, but great is preferred.

📖 **The way you feel:** Like a million dollars.

THE UNEXPECTED GIFTS OF 🎁
DRESSING SMART WITH EASY ELEGANCE

> What makes a man attractive? It's less about your face and body and more about your presence—the way you carry yourself when you walk into a room. Attitude, kindness, sense of humor, honesty, and charm are all part of the package. Some men are born wealthy, but no man is born with *elegance and class.* — JoAnna

What you will have when you *feel* like you look like a million dollars:

🎁 Confidence.

🎁 A job or a better job.

🎁 More credibility, respect, and authority.

🎁 Compliments from men and women.

🎁 Praise and a raise.

🎁 Notice and recognition.

🎁 A more secure future.

🎁 You'll feel *smart*, act *smart,* and you will be *smart*.

Contrary to what some experts advise, in a more casual workplace, clothes are MORE important than ever—what you are wearing sends a message to others about how you feel about yourself.

When you feel great about the way you look, you *interact* differently with **everyone,** and the impact of your self-assured behavior can touch many lives, especially your own.

Your truly extraordinary *gift* to others, and to yourself, is the positive radiating effect you can have on everyone whose life you touch and on those people whose lives they touch.

Beyond doubt, the way you feel about yourself will have an amazing impact on your life now (and your future), your family, your work performance, your co-workers, and the lives of the people they touch. When things go smoothly at work everyone has a more positive feeling about life and work in general—less stress brings more productivity and a better working environment for all. Co-workers, including your boss, go home happier, which happily impacts their relationships with the people in their lives.

Think about how your self-esteem affects your children, their happiness, the way they interact with you, their mother, and each other, and the way they behave and succeed at school. If a child is doing better in school, that adds to his or her self-confidence; that self-confidence inspires his/her teacher, affecting the teacher's work (with your child and all the others) and the teacher's home life, and so on, and the spiral continues.

When you feel confident about the way you look, your relationship with your significant other is more *delicious* (okay, maybe just better). But when you feel good about yourself, it's easier to show her how special you think she is and that makes her feel great. When *things* are better at home, she's different at work and that impacts on her job performance, her relationship with her boss, co-workers, and her co-workers' relationships with others. When her boss and co-workers are happier, she's happier at work and the circle comes back to you, touching your life, radiating out again, and so on, and, we hope someday, so goes the world.

Wishing you easy elegance and more personal and professional success than you dare to dream.
JoAnna

THE RESOURCE CENTER

JoAnna's websites
DressingSmart.com

- Take a free quiz to find your Dressing Smart I.Q.

- Order a *Mini Color Chart* to find your best colors of the season

- Print out your own Mini Chart in just a few minutes for just a few dollars

- Read articles about JoAnna's books in national magazines

Color1Associates.com

- Find the Color 1 Associate nearest you

- Take a free quiz to find your Color Type

- If you don't have an Associate near you, order the *Smart Chart*

- Change your career, change your life—click on Color 1 Careers

Career1Makeovers.com

- For the *smart* women in your life—you can order signed copies of JoAnna's book ***Dressing Smart for Women: 101 Mistakes You Can't Afford to Make & How to Avoid Them***. Send a separate email to JoAnna@DressingSmart.com with the name(s) you would like the book(s) signed to. All books are 25% off the retail price.

Sexy1Makeovers.com & Sexy1Makeup.com

- For the *smart* and *sexy* women in your life—you can order signed copies of JoAnna's book ***Secrets Men Have Told Me: What Turns Men On & What Turns Them Off***. Send a separate email to JoAnna@DressingSmart.com with the name(s) you would like the book(s) signed to. You'll get 25% off the retail price.

The *Smart* Chart
This full-sized chart, coupled with the information in this book, will be a great help to you in attaining the look you want. With at least one shade of every color in the spectrum that will flatter your Color Type, this chart is the *next* best thing to having a personal consultation with a Color 1 Associate. Take the free online quiz (visit Color1Associates.com) to help you

determine your Color Type—if you can't, you can send JoAnna a picture and she will do it for you.

The *Mini* Color Chart
Order this fun and helpful chart from the website if you are curious to know which of the latest "in-fashion" colors being shown in the stores each season are best for your Color Type. It's also available in a format that you can print out yourself—in just a few minutes, for just a few dollars. Take the free online quiz to help you figure out your Color Type.

Color 1 Associates International Image & Style Consultants
To "change the way the world looks at you" by working with one of the most talented, experienced, and most respected color and image consultants in the world, visit <u>Color1Associates.com</u>, or telephone Color 1 at (202) 293-9175, to find the Associate nearest you.

THE AUTHOR

President of Color 1 Associates, International Image & Style Consultants, JoAnna Nicholson is one of the founders of the image industry. She is a recipient of the prestigious Image Industry Council International (IICI) Award of Excellence and the IMMIE Award for Commitment.

JoAnna, the author of seven books, has trained image and style consultants all over the world. Lecturing internationally and nationally on color, style, wardrobe, makeup, and interior design, she has conducted seminars at the invitation of the American Embassy in Paris. Her television and radio appearances include the Montel Williams Show and the Larry King Show. She is a former model and co-founder of an interior design studio. Her home, which she designed using the Color 1 concept, has been featured in *Architectural Digest* and *Italian Architectural Digest.*

JoAnna's latest books are **Dressing Smart for Women: 101 Mistakes You Can't Afford to Make and How to Avoid Them** and **Secrets Men Have Told Me: What Turns Men On & What Turns Them Off**. Her company and books have been featured in numerous magazines including *Harper's Bazaar, GQ, Cosmopolitan, Glamour, Forbes, Black Elegance, Money,* and *Redbook*, and in over 100 newspapers including *The Washington Post*. Personal clients include ambassadors, cabinet secretaries, senators, congressmen, Fortune 500 companies, rock stars, actors, and a former Miss America.

CAREER RESOURCES

The following Career Resources are available directly from Impact Publications. Full descriptions of each title as well as downloadable catalogs, videos, and software can be found on our website: www.impactpublications.com. Complete the following form or list the titles, include shipping (see formula at the end), enclose payment, and send your order to:

IMPACT PUBLICATIONS
9104 Manassas Drive, Suite N
Manassas Park, VA 20111-5211 USA
1-800-361-1055 (orders only)
Tel. 703-361-7300 or Fax 703-335-9486
Email address: info@impactpublications.com
Quick & easy online ordering: www.impactpublications.com

Orders from individuals must be prepaid by check, money order, or major credit card. We accept telephone, fax, and email orders.

Qty.	Titles	Price	Total
Books By Author			
_____	Dressing Smart for Men	$16.95	_____
_____	Dressing Smart for Women	16.95	_____
_____	Dressing Smart for the New Millennium	15.95	_____
Networking			
_____	A Foot in the Door	14.95	_____
_____	Golden Rule of Schmoozing	12.95	_____
_____	How to Work a Room	14.00	_____
_____	Make Your Contacts Count	14.95	_____
_____	Masters of Networking	16.95	_____
_____	Power Networking	14.95	_____
_____	Power Schmoozing	12.95	_____
_____	The Savvy Networker	13.95	_____
_____	The Secrets of Savvy Networking	13.99	_____
Interviews			
_____	101 Dynamite Questions to Ask At Your Job Interview	13.95	_____
_____	Haldane's Best Answers to Tough Interview Questions	15.95	_____
_____	Interview for Success (8th Edition)	15.95	_____
_____	Interview Rehearsal Book	12.00	_____
_____	Job Interviews for Dummies	16.99	_____

Qty.	Title	Price	Total
_____	Nail the Job Interview	13.95	_____
_____	The Savvy Interviewer	10.95	_____

Salary Negotiations

Qty.	Title	Price	Total
_____	101 Salary Secrets	12.95	_____
_____	Better Than Money	18.95	_____
_____	Dynamite Salary Negotiations	15.95	_____
_____	Get a Raise in 7 Days	14.95	_____
_____	Haldane's Best Salary Tips for Professionals	15.95	_____

College-to-Career Resources

Qty.	Title	Price	Total
_____	101 Best Resumes for Grads	11.95	_____
_____	200 Best Jobs for College Graduates	16.95	_____
_____	America's Top Jobs for College Graduates	15.95	_____
_____	Best Resumes for College Students and New Grads	12.95	_____
_____	Great Careers in Two Years	19.95	_____
_____	A Fork in the Road: A Career Planning Guide for Young Adults	14.95	_____
_____	Gallery of Best Resumes for 2-Year Degree Graduates	18.95	_____
_____	Job Hunting Guide	14.95	_____

Assessment and Testing

Qty.	Title	Price	Total
_____	Career Tests	12.95	_____
_____	Discover the Best Jobs for You	15.95	_____
_____	Discover What You're Best At	14.00	_____
_____	Do What You Are	18.95	_____
_____	Finding Your Perfect Work	16.95	_____
_____	I Don't Know What I Want, But I Know It's Not This	14.95	_____
_____	Now, Discover Your Strengths	27.00	_____
_____	Pathfinder	15.00	_____
_____	What Type Am I?	14.95	_____
_____	What Should I Do With My Life?	24.95	_____
_____	What's Your Type of Career?	17.95	_____

Inspiration and Empowerment

Qty.	Title	Price	Total
_____	101 Secrets of Highly Effective Speakers	15.95	_____
_____	Eat That Frog!	19.95	_____
_____	Free the Beagle	14.95	_____
_____	Life Strategies	13.95	_____
_____	Seven Habits of Highly Effective People	14.00	_____
_____	Who Moved My Cheese?	19.95	_____

Career Exploration and Job Strategies

Qty.	Title	Price	Total
_____	50 Cutting Edge Jobs	15.95	_____

Qty.	Titles	Price	Total
_____	95 Mistakes Job Seekers Make	13.95	_____
_____	100 Great Jobs and How to Get Them	17.95	_____
_____	America's Top Jobs for People Without a Four-Year Degree	15.95	_____
_____	Best KeyWords for Resumes, Cover Letters, and Interviews	17.95	_____
_____	Career Change	14.95	_____
_____	Change Your Job, Change Your Life (8th Edition)	17.95	_____
_____	Directory of Executive Recruiters	49.95	_____
_____	High-Tech Careers for Low-Tech People	14.95	_____
_____	How to Get a Job and Keep It	16.95	_____
_____	Internships	26.95	_____
_____	Knock 'Em Dead	12.95	_____
_____	Me, Myself, and I, Inc.	17.95	_____
_____	No One Is Unemployable	29.95	_____
_____	No One Will Hire Me!	13.95	_____
_____	Occupational Outlook Handbook	16.95	_____
_____	Quit Your Job and Grow Some Hair	15.95	_____
_____	Rites of Passage at $100,000 to $1 Million+	29.95	_____
_____	What Color Is Your Parachute?	17.95	_____

Internet Job Search

Qty.	Titles	Price	Total
_____	America's Top Internet Job Sites	19.95	_____
_____	Guide to Internet Job Searching	14.95	_____
_____	Haldane's Best Employment Websites for Professionals	15.95	_____

Resumes and Letters

Qty.	Titles	Price	Total
_____	101 Great Tips for a Dynamite Resume	13.95	_____
_____	201 Dynamite Job Search Letters	19.95	_____
_____	Best Cover Letters for $100,000+ Jobs	24.95	_____
_____	Best Resumes and CVs for International Jobs	24.95	_____
_____	Best Resumes for $100,000+ Jobs	24.95	_____
_____	Haldane's Best Cover Letters for Professionals	15.95	_____
_____	Haldane's Best Resumes for Professionals	15.95	_____
_____	High Impact Resumes and Letters (8th Edition)	19.95	_____
_____	Military Resumes and Cover Letters	19.95	_____
_____	Resumes for Dummies	16.99	_____
_____	The Savvy Resume Writer	12.95	_____
_____	Sure-Hire Resumes	14.95	_____

International and Travel Jobs

Qty.	Titles	Price	Total
_____	Back Door Guide to Short-Term Job Adventures	21.95	_____
_____	Best Resumes and CVs for International Jobs	24.95	_____
_____	Directory of Websites for International Jobs	19.95	_____
_____	Flight Attendant Job Finder and Career Guide	16.95	_____
_____	Global Citizen	16.95	_____
_____	Global Resume and CV Guide	17.95	_____

Qty.	Title	Price	Total
_____	How to Get a Job in Europe (5th Edition)	22.95	_____
_____	Inside Secrets to Finding a Career in Travel	14.95	_____
_____	International Jobs (6th Edition)	19.00	_____
_____	International Job Finder	19.95	_____
_____	Jobs for Travel Lovers (4th Edition)	19.95	_____
_____	Teaching English Abroad	19.95	_____
_____	Work Abroad	15.95	_____
_____	Working Abroad	14.95	_____
_____	Work Your Way Around the World	19.95	_____

SUBTOTAL _____

Virginia residents add 4½% sales tax _____

POSTAGE/HANDLING ($5 for first product and 8% of SUBTOTAL) _____

8% of SUBTOTAL _____

TOTAL ENCLOSED _____

SHIP TO:

NAME _____

ADDRESS _____

_____

_____

PAYMENT METHOD:

❑ I enclose check/money order for $ _____ made payable to IMPACT PUBLICATIONS.

❑ Please charge $ _____ to my credit card:

❑ Visa   ❑ MasterCard   ❑ American Express ❑ Discover

Card # _____ Expiration date: ___ /___

Signature _____

Keep in Touch . . .
On the Web!

www.impactpublications.com
www.ishoparoundtheworld.com
www.hoteltravelshop.com
www.mycruiseshop.com
www.contentfortravel.com
www.winningthejob.com
www.veteransworld.com
www.contentforcareers.com